Palgrave Studies in Logistics and Supply Chain Management

Series Editors
Martin Christopher, School of Management, Cranfield University, Cranfield, Beds., UK
Emel Aktas, School of Management, Building 32, Cranfield University, Cranfield, UK

Logistics and supply chain management has always been critical to business success and to the efficient running of economies and the well-being of the societies they serve. In recent years, however, the importance of these activities has been highlighted by geopolitical challenges and uncertainty that have threatened global supply chains.

The series provides an opportunity to explore in-depth and with rigour topics such as digital transformation, supply chain risk and resilience, sustainability and the circular economy, and the future of global supply chain design and management. Entries in the series are international in outlook, providing fresh and innovative approaches to pressing issues in logistics and supply chain management.

Carla Pereira · Öznur Yurt

Achieving Resilience in Service Supply Chains

The Role of Procurement

palgrave
macmillan

Carla Pereira
Department of People
and Organisations
The Open University
Milton Keynes, UK

Öznur Yurt
Department of People
and Organisations
The Open University
Milton Keynes, UK

Department of Logistics Management
Izmir University of Economics
Izmir, Turkey

Palgrave Studies in Logistics and Supply Chain Management
ISBN 978-3-031-68243-8 ISBN 978-3-031-68244-5 (eBook)
https://doi.org/10.1007/978-3-031-68244-5

This Palgrave Macmillan imprint is published by the registered company Springer Nature Switzerland AG
The registered company address is: Gewerbestrasse 11, 6330 Cham, Switzerland

Acknowledgements

We would like to express our deepest gratitude to all those who contributed to the development of this study, making it possible.

We extend our special thanks to the Editors, Emeritus Prof. Dr. Martin Christopher and Prof. Dr. Emel Aktas, for their invaluable support and insightful suggestions throughout the creation of this Pivot. We are particularly grateful to Professor Dr. Martin Christopher for his guidance, mentorship, and encouragement throughout our academic and professional journeys.

We would also like to acknowledge the unwavering encouragement and academic support provided by Prof. Dr. Andrea Lago da Silva, Prof. Dr. Wendy Tate, and Prof. Dr. Tunçdan Baltacioğlu during our time as PhD students. Their support laid the foundation for the continuation and further development of this study.

We also thank Palgrave Macmillan and the support staff for the opportunity to publish this work, which is part of our academic interests and expertise.

Finally, we extend our appreciation to our readers. It is our sincere hope that this book offers valuable insights and makes a meaningful contribution to your practice as students, academics, or practitioners in the field of service procurement aiming to achieve supply chain resilience.

With sincere gratitude,

Carla Pereira
Öznur Yurt

Contents

About the Authors

Carla Pereira is a Lecturer in Operations & Supply Chain Management at The Open University Business School, United Kingdom. She holds a B.Eng. (2008) degree in Production Engineering (focused on agroindustry) from the State University of Maringá (Brazil) and MSc (2011) and PhD (2014) degrees in Production Engineering from the Federal University of São Carlos (Brazil), with exchange studies at Cranfield University (School of Management), United Kingdom. Carla's research and teaching interests include different topics in supply chain management (such as food waste, service, sustainability, and resilience), procurement/purchasing, and lean thinking (construction, manufacturing, distribution, healthcare, and office). She was the prior coordinator of the research group in the supply chain (Núcleo de Estudos e Pesquisa in Supply Chain) at UDESC. Additionally, Dr. Pereira is a Visiting Lecturer at the Post-Graduation Program in Civil Engineering at UDESC, where she supervises students in the area of urban resilience and lean construction and teaches modules on systematic literature review methodology and paper development. Research outcomes have been published in several journals, including the International Journal of Production Economics, Waste Management, and Supply Chain Management: an International Journal.

Öznur Yurt is a Senior Lecturer in Operations & Supply Chain Management at The Open University Business School, United Kingdom. She is also an Adjunct Professor of Marketing and Supply Chain Management at the Izmir University of Economics, Turkey. She holds two PhDs from the Izmir University of Economics in Turkey and from the University of Miskolc (Hungary). She conducted her postdoctoral studies at the Cranfield School of Management and the University of Plymouth. Prior to joining academia, she worked in the banking industry in Turkey. Her research interests include service supply chains, procurement management, business-to-business marketing, food supply chains, and supply chain resilience. Her work has been published in journals such as the *International Journal of Operations & Production Management, Industrial Marketing Management, Production Planning & Control, Supply Chain Management: An International Journal, European Journal of Marketing, Service Industries Journal, Journal of Service Theory and Practice, The Service Industries Journal, and Resources, Conservation & Recycling.*

List of Figures

List of Tables

CHAPTER 1

Introduction

Abstract Chapter 1 introduces the key concepts explored in the pivot—service operations management, procurement management, and supply chain resilience—in a way that brings their currency and importance to today's service businesses. It aims to address the intersection of these concepts by examining the role of procurement management, particularly service procurement, in achieving resilience in service supply chains. It also provides an overview of the content of the book (clarifying the content covered in each chapter) and presents the foundation of this book through the work of the authors.

Keywords Service supply chains · Procurement management · Supply chain resilience

In today's increasingly service-oriented global economy, there has been significant growth in activities and transactions within and between organisations in the service sector (Arlbjørn et al., 2011; Enz & Lambert, 2023; Giannakis, 2011). This leads to various changes in our lives, including technological advancements, disruptive events from various sources, and volatile markets where customers are more demanding and exhibit constantly changing spending patterns. By 2035, the service sector

C. Pereira and Ö. Yurt, *Achieving Resilience in Service Supply Chains*, Palgrave Studies in Logistics and Supply Chain Management,
https://doi.org/10.1007/978-3-031-68244-5_1

is projected to constitute 77% of global GDP1 (UK government, 2023). In particular, some specific service sectors play a significant role in shaping the UK economy. Tourism, for instance, is a major industry within the service sector in the UK. In 2022, tourists spent more than £26.5 billion, marking a significant increase from the previous year, primarily due to the lifting of travel restrictions imposed during the pandemic (Page & Brown, 2023).

At the same time, global risks and disruptions have altered the way organisations manage and run their businesses. According to the Scottish Financial News (2024), firms' annual risk reports indicate that business leaders are facing severe disruptions. Although they tend to perceive such risks in a negative way and seek alternatives to minimise them, there are also potential opportunities for them to obtain a competitive advantage by responding positively to challenging conditions. This is just an example of why and how the concept of resilience has become vital for both researchers and practitioners. Resilience, particularly in the context of a supply chain, has been considered a key capability for managers aiming to thrive in the face of a volatile environment and dynamic market.

Considering these issues, there has been increasing interest from both scholars and practitioners in topics such as "service operations management", "procurement management", and "supply chain resilience". However, research at the intersection of these three important and developing concepts is still scarce. Therefore, we aim to address this gap by answering the following question in this book: *What is the role of procurement management, particularly service procurement, in achieving resilience in service supply chains?* To address this question, the three aforementioned concepts are introduced separately before connecting them.

In Chapter 2, the concept of service is introduced, with a particular focus on the complex nature of supply chain interconnections and the unexpected and disruptive events that affect them. This chapter begins by highlighting some of the most common disruptions in recent years and discussing trends for the future. It then explains the concept of service as a product and expands this concept by introducing the service industry. Finally, the chapter explains the service supply chain through different models and highlights some of the challenges faced by service supply chain (SSC) members during disruptive events.

In Chapter 3, the concept of procurement is first introduced, covering its evolution and terminology differences. It then emphasises the main areas of managing resources, the responsibilities of a procurement team, and how it acts as a boundary-spanning function. Considering the role of "humans" in procurement, the chapter highlights some skills and competencies. Additionally, it reflects on service supply chain professionals and the relation between service procurement and procurement in the service supply chain.

In Chapter 4, the concept of resilience is discussed, shedding light on its key meaning within the areas of operations and supply chain management (O&SCM). In doing so, this paper discusses the three perspectives of resilience (engineering, ecological, and social-ecological), the bundle of elements of resilience, and how risk and vulnerability are interrelated concepts of resilience. The chapter ends by providing a range of examples of resilience in the service industry and supply chain.

In Chapter 5, we delve into the particularities of service, procurement, and resilience to understand how service supply chain resilience can be achieved through procurement actions classified into intraorganisational domains (knowledge and skills, inventory, service as solutions, and technology) and interorganisational domains (strategic sourcing, service supply chain design, transportation, and risk in service). Practical outcomes and examples from interviews conducted with professionals in service supply chain members, such as hotels, airline companies, and third-party logistics firms, are used to provide a better understanding of the domains.

Finally, Chapter 6 revisits the key domains discussed in Chapter 5, together with key insights from the other chapters, to offer practical highlights and guidelines on how procurement management can support service professionals in better managing their supply chain processes and making their systems more resilient. These domains are the basis for procurement to efficiently oversee and synchronise the flow of services, materials, information, and related activities.

Figure 1.1 illustrates the overall structure taken to develop the content of this pivot.

This pivot brings new knowledge to service procurement processes, enabling professionals and researchers to gain a deeper understanding of the intricacies involved in managing service supply chains. The guidelines and recommendations provided by this pivot are not only informative but also inspiring service businesses to enhance their competitiveness, improve their performance, and effectively navigate the ever-evolving landscape of the service industry.

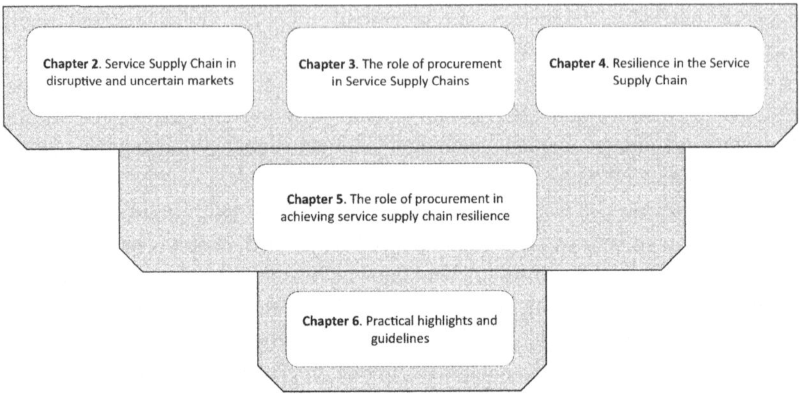

Fig. 1.1 Pivot Structure

The content of this pivot had its starting point on the outcomes from our PhD studies—"The Role of Procurement in Achieving Supply Chain Resilience" (Pereira, 2014) and "The Impact of Services Supply Chain Orientation on Perceived Industrial Service Quality: An Empirical Analysis" (Yurt, 2007). Pereira (2014) explored how procurement managers within manufacturing organisations can address intra- and interorganisational issues and, consequently, promote resilience through their actions. This work has evolved from a particular focus on procurement in the manufacturing sector to the service sector, considering the importance of this industry looking forward and how the findings and outcomes from the manufacturing side could form the basis for actions in the service industry. Over the past 10 years, Dr. Pereira has developed her studies in a more in-depth way by exploring the concept of resilience from different perspectives in operations and supply chain management (O&SCM) but mostly by looking at food waste and surplus. On the other hand, the work of Yurt (2007) highlights the growing importance of "service supply chains", with a particular focus on "service supply chain orientation" and "service quality". Since then, Dr. Yurt's research has focused on different aspects of the supply chain, mainly from the perspective of service operations and supply chains, such as supply chain risk management and resilience, integrated solutions, and service modularity. Her research outputs provide a strong basis for this pivot, particularly regarding the ideas for defining, designing, and managing service procurement actions and strategies for suppliers, providers, and customers from a service supply chain viewpoint. This inclusive perspective allows for a complete understanding of the service supply chain's interconnected relationships, collaborative activities, and interdependence (Yildirim et al., 2018; Yurt & Yildirim, 2022).

We believe that this pivot is a timely resource for a wide range of individuals, including researchers, students, educators, professional trainers, supply chain leaders, and professionals in procurement management, supply chain management, or any service business. Examples and insights identified in the literature and those also shared by practitioners, especially after COVID-19, and conflicts of different natures (from environmental disasters to recent geopolitical tensions and wars) provide a comprehensible understanding and awareness of the current digital era, in which every professional inevitably realises that an increasing portion of their business is becoming a service.

Finally, we hope that readers will find this book insightful and helpful for their study and practice.

References

Arlbjørn, J. S., Freytag, P. V., & Haas, H. (2011). Service supply chain management: A survey of lean application in the municipal sector. *International Journal of Physical Distribution & Logistics Management, 41*(3), 277–295.

Enz, M. G., & Lambert, D. M. (2023). A supply chain management framework for services. *Journal of Business Logistics, 44*(1), 11–36.

Giannakis, M. (2011). Conceptualizing and managing service supply chains. *The Service Industries Journal, 31*(11), 1809–1823.

Page, V. & Brown, J.R. (2023). The Economy of the United Kingdom. *Investopedia*. Investopedia International Markets, 11 August 2023. Web. Retrieved from: https://www.investopedia.com/articles/investing/042915/how-uk-makes-money.asp#:~:text=The%20services%20sector%E2%80%94which%20comprises,construction%20account%20for%20about%2016%25

Pereira, C. R., Christopher, M., & Silva, A. L. (2014). Achieving supply chain resilience: The role of procurement. *Supply Chain Management: An International Journal, 19*(5/6), 626–642.

Pereira, C. R. (2014). *The Role of Procurement in Creating Supply Chain Resilience* (PhD thesis). Federal University of Sao Carlos, Sao Carlos, Brazil. Available at: https://repositorio.ufscar.br/handle/ufscar/3451 (Last accessed: 31.05.2024).

Scottish Financial News. (2024). BDO: Businesses must adapt or fail in crisis-defined landscape. Retrieved from https://www.scottishfinancialnews.com/articles/bdo-84-of-business-leaders-see-global-risk-at-all-time-high (Last accessed: 22.06.2024).

UK Government. (2023). Global Trade Outlook-February 2023: *Executive Summary*. Retrieved from https://www.gov.uk/government/publications/global-trade-outlook-february-2023-report/global-trade-outlook-february-2023-html-executive-summary#:~:text=By%202035%2C%20service%20sectors%20are,key%20source%20of%20demand%20growth

Yurt, O., & Yildirim, C. (2022). Exploring integrated solutions in the supply chain context: A dyadic perspective in an emerging economy setting. *Production Planning & Control, 35*(1), 21–45.

Yildirim, C., Oflaç, B. S., & Yurt, O. (2018). The doer effect of failure and recovery in multi-agent cases: Service supply chain perspective. *Journal of Service Theory and Practice, 28*(3), 274–297.

Yurt, O. (2007). *The impact of services supply chain orientation on perceived industrial service quality: An empirical analysis* (PhD thesis). Izmir University of Economics, Izmir, Turkey. Available at: https://tez.yok.gov.tr/UlusalTezMerkezi/tezSorguSonucYeni.jsp (Last accessed: 01.05.2024).

CHAPTER 2

Service Supply Chains in Disruptive and Uncertain Markets

Abstract In Chapter 2, the concept of service is introduced, with a particular focus on the complex nature of supply chain interconnections and the unexpected and disruptive events that affect them. This chapter begins by highlighting some of the most common disruptions in recent years and discussing trends for the future. It then explains the concept of service as a product and expands this concept by introducing the service industry. Finally, the chapter explains the service supply chain through different models and highlights some of the challenges faced by service supply chain (SSC) members during disruptive events.

Keywords Service concept · Disruptions · Service sector · Service supply chains

This chapter aims to provide a comprehensive understanding of the service concept, its evolution, and its critical role in the economy. Furthermore, we offer insights into recent disruptions in global supply chains in the context of service to provide a basis for the current market and business challenges discussed at the end of this chapter.

C. Pereira and Ö. Yurt, *Achieving Resilience in Service Supply Chains*, Palgrave Studies in Logistics and Supply Chain Management,
https://doi.org/10.1007/978-3-031-68244-5_2

2.1 Recent Disruptions in Global Supply Chains

The dynamic and disruptive nature of global markets and the exposure of supply chains to various risks have long been a focal point of academic research (e.g., Christopher & Holweg, 2011; Christopher et al., 2011; Gurbuz et al., 2023). This subject has not only attracted scholarly attention but also become a paramount concern for industry practitioners, particularly in the wake of the negative consequences linked to hundreds of natural and man-made disruptions in the flow of goods and services throughout supply chains. However, especially after 2020, in the aftermath of the COVID-19 pandemic, all businesses (regardless of their sector or size) were compelled to have more caution in their decision-making processes since their decisions directly or indirectly affected others throughout the global supply chain system, creating a snowballing effect.

Currently, events such as natural disasters, wars, political turmoil, pandemics, macroeconomic fluctuations, cyberattacks, infrastructure breakdowns, power outages, strike actions, and employee turnover constitute some of the various sources of disruptions that impact several supply chains. As the word "disruption" has been used frequently in different contexts, especially after COVID-19, we would like to present a definition on which we base our discussions. We understand supply chain disruptions as *"...unplanned and unanticipated events that disrupt the normal flow of goods and materials within a supply chain"* (Craighead et al., 2007, p.132). Although it focuses on the flow of goods and materials, we build on this definition by emphasising how "service flow" has been affected by such disruptions in the following sections.

The wide impact of unforeseen events, such as the COVID-19 pandemic, the Suez Canal blockage in March 2021, and ongoing political conflicts such as Ukraine–Russia and Israel–Hamas, has reminded us of the importance of understanding the supply chain as a system. This has led to a more careful consideration of risks, vulnerabilities, and key areas of management (e.g., careful selection of partners, production capacity, inventory, and location of facilities). These events have also influenced the recognition and categorisation of risks (Crawford & Jabbour, 2024; Jüttner et al., 2003; Naeini & Badri, 2024). While there are numerous global risk categorisations provided in the literature to date, the "The Global Risk Report" proposed by the World Economic Forum (2024) offers a comprehensive classification of global risks into economic, environmental, geopolitical, societal, and technological. Figure 2.1 provides a visual representation of the current global risk landscape based on survey results reflecting people's perceptions of global risks, ranked by severity over the short and long term.

The risks outlined in that report, especially in the long term, involve escalating environmental concerns, particularly those related to climate change and nature. These risks encompass challenges such as the failure to address climate change, crises in natural resource availability (e.g., soil degradation, water quality decline), pervasive cybercrime and insecurity in the digital realm (e.g., the 2017 NotPetya cyberattack in Ukraine affected global supply chain members, including the shipping giant Maersk), geoeconomic confrontations (e.g., the US–China trade war), and large-scale incidents causing environmental damage (e.g., Brazilian Amazon deforestation). The report also highlights emerging or rapidly intensifying risks to natural ecosystems, human health, security, digital rights, and economic stability, which could evolve into crises and catastrophes in the coming decades (The World Economic Forum, 2024).

One can think of why such unexpected situations, dynamism, volatility, disruptions, and, ultimately, risks are particularly important in the context

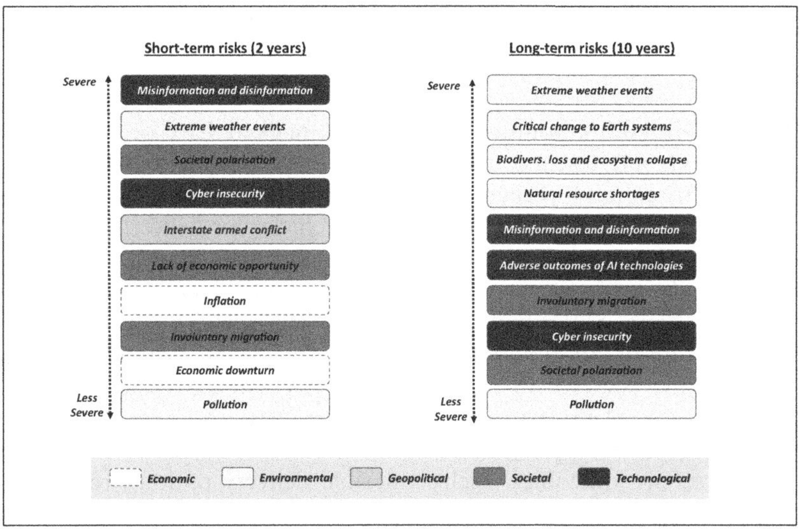

Fig. 2.1 A global risk category ranked by severity over the short and long term
Source: Adapted from the World Economic Forum (2024)

of supply chains. Our simple and straightforward answer would be the growing interconnection among companies that causes network complexity in the current global sourcing scenario (Pereira et al., 2014). The reason for highlighting "global sourcing" at this point is that only a very small number of businesses today do not have supply chain members across different countries. In this context, we particularly consider and call attention to their impacts on service flows in supply chains. Therefore, let us first gain a better understanding of service as a product and the dynamics of the service industry.

2.2 Service as a Product and the Service Industry

In today's ever-changing global service sector, the traditional distinctions between tangible products and intangible services are becoming increasingly blurred, creating a seamless continuum. This ongoing transformation brings together a level of uncertainty in which the interplay between services and physical products challenges both industry professionals and researchers.

The question of "what the service is" evolving into "what service is in it" reflects the growing significance of services for all businesses. In alignment with this perspective and with a notable focus on service-dominant logic (SDL) proposed by Vargo and Lusch (2004), the definition and role of services in both consumer and industrial markets have been the focal points of ongoing discussion in the literature (Sampson, 2000).

The SDL concept challenges the traditional product-centric view by proposing that all products are essentially vehicles for delivering services. This view led to a transformation of our understanding and posited that all supply chains must prioritise the management of service flows along the entire chain. SDL emphasises the customer involvement and experiential nature of consumption, suggesting that the service provider and the consumer cocreate value. From this perspective, products are only instruments or platforms that enable the provision of services. In the context of service, supply chain activities should be aligned with delivering superior service outcomes, such as flexible delivery options, responsive customer service, and personalised offerings. This is why supply chain integration and collaboration are critical, particularly for service supply chain members to be able to cocreate value with customers. On the other hand, the adaptability and agility of service supply chain members play a significant role in responding to changing customer demands and market conditions. This viewpoint emphasises the significance of customer centricity, integration, agility, and sustainability in the management of supply chains. Adopting SDL offers significant opportunities for businesses to create more value for their customers and gain competitive advantages in today's dynamic marketplace. Due to the potential for enhanced responsiveness, resilience, and responsibility in supply chains that better address customer needs, we focused our discussion on the adoption of SDL principles throughout this pivot.

Additionally, we highlight that the provision of goods in service sectors (e.g., the supply of bedding materials in the tourism sector) is our indirect focus on this pivot. However, we keep our discussion focused on the settings where organisations provide services to each other, such as the supply of entertainment services to a full-inclusive resort hotel. It is critical to emphasise that service supply chains are not entirely distinct from traditional ones but rather encompass core service elements and processes (Sampson & Spring, 2012b).

As Christopher (2023, p. 235) stated, "...the more that the distinction between products and services becomes blurred, and the more that clients and customers demand customised solutions, then the more the value delivery process comes to resemble a project". This, in the context of services, means that supply chains can even be considered "projects". Furthermore, Fitzsimmons and Fitzsimmons (2006, p.31) mentioned, *"for services, the process is the product"*. However, before we proceed with our discussion on service as a product in the context of supply chain management, let us develop a more detailed reflection on the service concept.

2.2.1 The Concept of Service

To start exploring the essence of service, let us look at some definitions of service in the literature (Table 2.1).

Given that service marketing, service management, and service operations are well-developed fields of study, the definitions above are not recent. However, service has been studied in different contexts by reflecting from various perspectives. This pivot is one example of such an attempt.

Table 2.1 Definitions of service

Authors	*Service definition*
Grönroos (1990, p.27)	*A service is an activity or series of activities of more or less intangible nature that normally, but not necessarily, take place in interactions between customer and service employees and/or physical resources or goods and/or systems of the service provider, which are provided as solutions to customer problems*
Zeithaml et al., (2006, p.4)	*Services are deeds, processes, and performances*
Fitzsimmons and Fitzsimmons (2006, p.4)	*A service is a time-perishable, intangible experience performed for a customer acting in the role of coproducer*
Johnston and Clark, (2005, p.10)	*...the combination of outcomes and experiences delivered to and received by a customer*
Wirtz and Lovelock (2018, p. 14)	*Services are economic activities between two parties, implying an exchange of value between the seller and the buyer in the marketplace*

The service concept can be effectively explained by highlighting the distinctions between "physical products" and "services". "Physical products" pertain to the advantages derived from owning physical objects or devices, while "services" involve the benefits generated through actions or performances (Wirtz & Lovelock, 2018). It is important to recognise that a company's offering may encompass a pure service, a tangible good, or a blend of both.

Now, let us emphasise the distinctive characteristics of goods and services. Fundamentally, a good (as a physical product) constitutes a tangible product that can be manufactured, transferred from its origin to the consumption point, and stored for future use. In contrast, a service is intangible, perishable, and must be produced concurrently (Bruhn & Georgi, 2006; Wirtz & Lovelock, 2018).

Identifying the differences between a good and a service might not be easy or straightforward. For instance, when a physical good is bought, that purchase includes some services such as after-sales support and warranties. Similarly, when a service is purchased, it might be accompanied by certain products, such as restaurant food or hotel accommodations. Therefore, each purchase comprises a bundle of goods and services known as a "service package", as suggested by Fitzsimmons and Fitzsimmons (2006). This bundle is shown in Table 2.2.

As a further clarification, Table 2.3 provides a generic table on different aspects of purchasing goods and services.

Table 2.2 Service and product bundle *Source: Adapted from* Fitzsimmons & Fitzsimmons, 2006

Element	*Core goods examples*	*Core services examples*
Business	Custom clothier	Business hotel
Core	Business suits	Room for the night
Peripheral goods	Garment bag	Bathrobe
Peripheral services	Deferred payment plans	In-house restaurant
Variant	Coffee lounge	Airport shuttle

Table 2.3 Purchasing goods versus services *Source: Adapted from* Allen and Chandrashekar (2000)

Aspect	*Goods*	*Services*
Expectations	Have clear and precise specifications	Usually, it consists of unclear service level agreements
Risk Management	Quality is measurable and prespecified	Quality is dependent upon the user and subjectively determined
Predictability of Demand	Depends upon the forecast and the needs of the end customer	Varies with the scope of the project
Cost	Cost is prenegotiated by individual unit	Cost fluctuates depending upon the changing scope and requirements
Verification of Completion	Products are physically present and can be verified upon receipt	Requires an internal sign-off completion, unable to verify services performed
Payment	Verifiable with a three-way match: invoice, receiving document, and purchase order	There is little tangible evidence, and often pay-as-you-go

The differences mentioned above highlight the necessity for a proper and updated conceptualisation of the service supply chain. In the next sections, we will explore these differences thoroughly when defining the service supply chain.

While the fundamental distinctions have been outlined, determining a precise boundary between a physical product and a service is challenging and unnecessary. When an end-user buys a physical product, additional services such as after-sales support and warranties are often included. Likewise, the purchase of a service often entails the provision of certain goods, such as food at a restaurant or a bed in a hotel. Consequently, every purchase comprises a combination of goods and services, referred to as a "service package" (Fitzsimmons & Fitzsimmons, 2006), as previously explained.

The flower of service model (Fig. 2.2), proposed by Wirtz and Lovelock (2018, p. 95), provides a strong basis for defining the nature of a service offering by giving particular importance to two components: the core service and supplementary services. The core service refers to the core set of benefits and solutions delivered to customers, whereas supplementary services are the variety of service-related activities surrounding the core service (facilitating elements and enhancing elements). In this sense, supplementary services either facilitate service delivery to the customer (e.g., payment, billing, order taking, information) or enhance it by adding extra value for customers (e.g., consultation, hospitality, safekeeping, exceptions).

This model provides a comprehensive approach to service design and delivery by incorporating both core and supplementary services. The flower symbolises that the core service is central to the offering, while the supplementary services work as petals that surround and support it, creating a complete and attractive package for customers. This model helps service providers understand the full scope of their offerings and how each component contributes to overall customer satisfaction and value. The visualisation of the model as a flower signifies that while the core service is at the heart of the offering, the petals (supplementary service-facilitating and enhancing services) surround and support it, creating a complete bundle for customers. Facilitating services ensure that the service is accessible to the customer, whereas enhancing services improves the customer experience.

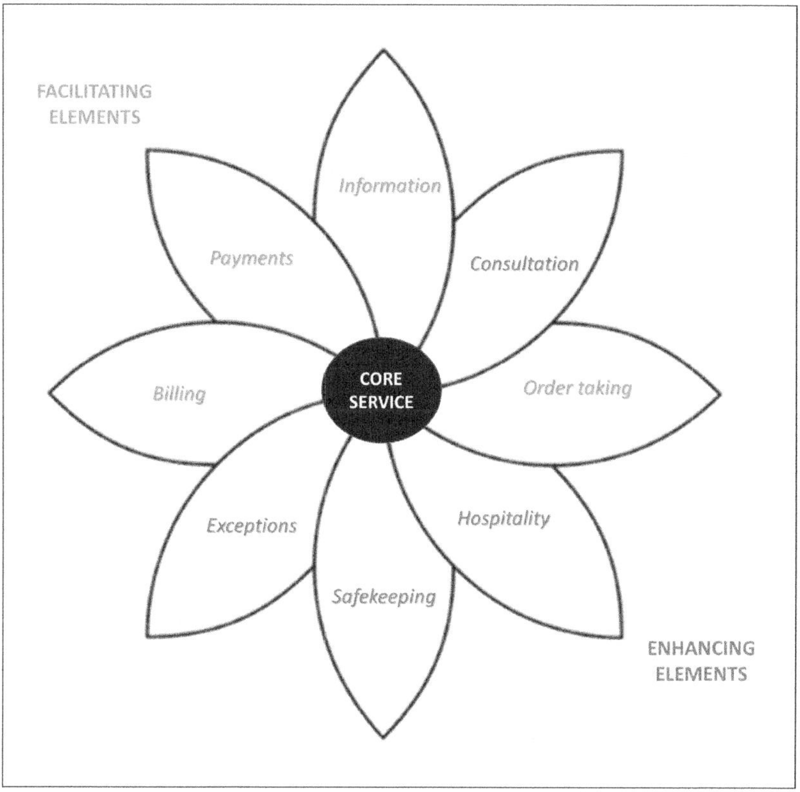

Fig. 2.2 The flower of service *Source: Adapted from* Wirtz and Lovelock (2018, *p. 95)*

The main logic in this model is that a successfully executed service design requires both the core of the flower and all relevant petals to be well-formed and fresh.

2.2.2 *The Service Sector*

Recently, the service sector has undergone significant growth in size, diversity, and complexity. In 2023, the service industry in the UK comprised 4.2 million businesses, accounting for slightly more than 75%

of all businesses. In general, service industries constitute 80% of employment and 72% of overall turnover (Hutton, 2024). This expansion is largely attributed to technological advancements, increased global trade, and a heightened emphasis on specialisation.

Factors such as unexpected crises, disasters, technological innovations, digitalisation, and societal shifts generate demand for various new services or new types of service designs. As economic growth requires new services, service companies regularly introduce new offers, significantly contributing to the expansion of the service industry. Consequently, the number of companies and individuals choosing to procure services from service businesses continues to rise, as highlighted in Chapter 1.

As the global economy continues to evolve, there has been a significant shift in the proportion of employment in service industries. The output of the service industry now makes up a substantial portion of the GDP, not only in developed countries but also in emerging economies. The UK serves as a prime example of this trend (Statista, 2024). The modern economy is largely driven by the service sector, and changes within this industry directly impact our daily lives and work habits. In addition to meeting existing consumer needs, new service areas are emerging to address needs that have not yet been recognised by the public. As a result, the number and size of service organisations are steadily increasing, leading to heightened competition within the industry.

Digital platforms have been rapidly transforming traditional business models, enabling on-demand access to services and goods, a phenomenon known as "uberification". This terminology is a reflection of a technological innovation that enhances a new way of providing service in the transportation sector. Platforms such as Netflix, YouTube, and Apple Music are pioneering examples of this. Additionally, Airbnb, TaskRabbit, and Fiverr are other examples of platforms that follow similar logic in several sectors, which also led to a shift from ownership models to subscription-based services. Although we will delve into the details in the following sections, we would like to mention that these changes are reshaping supply chains, emphasising flexibility, efficiency, and customer centricity, particularly in the context of service. As technology continues to evolve, supply chains will increasingly leverage digital tools to meet the demands of a rapidly changing market. However, as a starting point, let us first focus on the classification of services.

Services can be classified in different ways. For example, The WTO and The World Bank (2024) provide a clear classification of the service sector into different subsectors. The services listed in the report of The WTO and The World Bank (2024) are as follows:

- Business services
- Communication services
- Construction and related engineering services
- Distribution services
- Educational services
- Environmental services
- Financial services
- Health-related and social services
- Tourism and travel-related services
- Recreational, cultural and sporting services
- Transport services
- Other services not included elsewhere.

Aligned with the fact that the world economy is becoming increasingly service-oriented, the activities and transactions of service businesses within and between various entities have become significantly important (Arlbjørn et al., 2011; Giannakis, 2011; Wang et al., 2015). Additionally, the increasing relevance of the service industry has accelerated the attention of academics since the early 1980s. Scholarly work during this period primarily focused on delineating the differences between service and manufacturing businesses. Consequently, services marketing and service management have become prominent topics in the literature.

The increasing interest was primarily fuelled by the distinct features of services, such as perishability, intangibility, simultaneity, and heterogeneity (Zeithaml et al., 2006). Nevertheless, it is essential to note that, in addition to these distinctive features, there are other areas in the literature and models that require analysis, revision, and implementation for the service business, such as "service supply chains" (SSCs).

2.3 Service in the Context of a Supply Chain

The significance of service within a supply chain can be examined from various perspectives. Traditionally, "service" has been highlighted as a critical element that must be efficiently managed throughout the entire supply chain. While many prominent supply chain studies have acknowledged the importance of the service flow, its role is often depicted as supportive or secondary. However, some researchers have highlighted the importance of service in the definitions of supply chain management in their seminal works (e.g., Christopher, 1992; Mentzer et al., 2001), where they provided a basis for the concept of "service supply chains".

> *"...the network of organizations that are involved, through upstream and downstream linkages, in different processes and activities that produce value in the form of products and services in the hands of ultimate consumer." (*Christopher, 1992*)*
>
> *"...the integration of key business processes from end user through original suppliers that provides products, services, and information that add value for customers and other stakeholders." (*Lambert et al., in conjunction with the Global Supply Chain Forum, 1998*)*
>
> *"... a set of three or more entities (organizations or individuals) directly involved in the upstream and downstream flows of products, services, finances, and/or information from a source to a customer." (*Mentzer et al., 2001*)*

Although the significance of services in the business-to-consumer context has been extensively documented, there remains a notable gap in understanding the critical role of service exchanges within and between businesses in industrial markets, an area that has received relatively less attention. The onset of COVID-19 has significantly reshaped industry challenges, directing research focus towards the role of services within supply chains and resulting in substantial research outputs (e.g., Walletzký et al., 2023). Consequently, the importance of services in the global economy and within global supply chains has become increasingly apparent to both practitioners and academics. This recognition has spurred efforts to better understand the integration of services in supply chain contexts and the development of service supply chains (e.g., Arlbjørn et al., 2011; Ellram et al., 2004; Giannakis, 2011; Wang et al., 2015).

Despite these advances, the body of work on service supply chains remains relatively limited. Nevertheless, although we do not go into the details of the bundles of services and physical products that are used by organisations as a tool to support their supply chain partners in solving their business problems, there is extensive and ever-evolving research on this business strategy. The terms that are related to this rich field of research are servitisation, integrated solutions, and product-service

systems (Neely et al., 2011; Rapaccini & Visintin, 2015; Tuli et al., 2007)
.

2.3.1 *Development of the Service Supply Chain*

Following the views of Lusch (2011), we advocate for a shift in research on supply chain management from a dominant traditional view to a service-oriented one. Over time, the literature has emphasised the dynamics of supply chain networks, particularly those involving service businesses, often referred to as service supply chains. Consequently, the role of services in supply chains has become more visible for practitioners and has received increasing attention from researchers (e.g., Sampson & Spring, 2012a; Wang et al., 2015; Zhang & Chen, 2015).

Before delving into the specifics of practices, it is important to establish a clear definition of "service supply chain management". Previous studies have sought to grasp the nature and structure of service supply chains, presenting alternative definitions (e.g., Baltacioglu et al., 2007; Ellram et al., 2004). Some investigations have explored the feasibility of applying manufacturing supply chain practices to the realm of services (e.g., Cook et al., 2002; Kathawala & Abdou, 2003). Additionally, as mentioned earlier, research has delved into related concepts such as service supply management (e.g., Ellram et al., 2004) and the integration of physical products and services, such as product-service systems (e.g., Tukker, 2004), servitisation (e.g., Baines & Lightfoot, 2013), manufacturing service integration (e.g., Schmenner, 2009), and integrated solutions/offerings (e.g., Tuli et al., 2007). These studies provide diverse perspectives for understanding service supply chains.

The groundbreaking study of Ellram et al. (2004) made a significant and innovative impact on the service supply chain field. The authors presented a comprehensive framework for service supply chains, emphasising the critical service processes that occur throughout the supply chain. This framework was adapted from the literature on supply chain management in manufacturing, which highlights the essential service processes and functions. Figure 2.3 visually represents information flow as a central component of their framework.

Emphasising the need to tailor the concept of supply chain management to the service business and acknowledging the structural disparities between goods and services, Baltacioglu et al., (2007, p. 112) proposed one of the initial definitions of service supply chains:

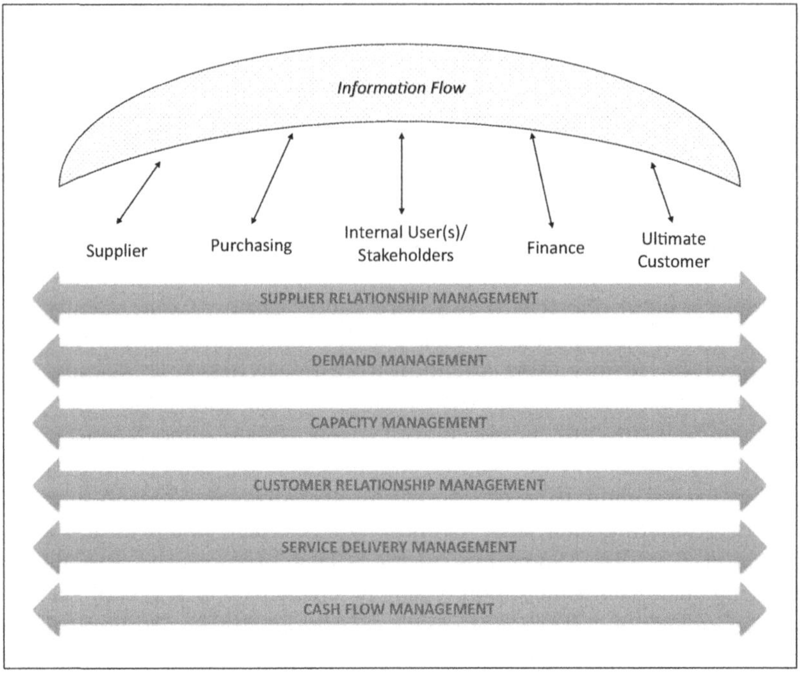

Fig. 2.3 Service Supply Chain Model *Source: Authors generated based on* Ellram et al. (2004)

> *"...the network of suppliers, service providers, consumers and other supporting units that performs the functions of transaction of resources required to produce services; transformation of these resources into supporting and core services; and the delivery of these services to customers."*

They also proposed a framework for service supply chain management, as depicted in Fig. 2.4. The main concept in this figure is to tailor the unique characteristics of services to the notion of supply chain management. The figure was devised by taking into account the intangibility (which makes it impractical to apply all logistics activities to a traditional supply chain structure), simultaneity (the reason for the challenge in managing service operations and inventorying services), heterogeneity (which heightens the complexity in planning and analysing service operations as well as in measuring the output), perishability (making services impossible to store in a warehouse), and the importance of the human aspect (requiring the acknowledgement of human resources as a core function rather than a supporting one) (Balouei Jamkhaneh et al., 2023; Baltacioglu et al., 2007; Ellram, et al. 2007; Nie & Kellogg, 1999).

The central concept of service supply chain management revolves around the idea that the ultimate product provided to the customer is the "core service" delivering value to them. Assets such as materials, financial resources, human resources, technological assets, and information or knowledge can be traded between businesses along the supply chain. In the service industry, the primary exchange factor is the service itself, making the service flow the core flow along the service supply chain.

While delivering a core service, additional supporting services may be necessary. Examples include staying in a hotel, attending a theatre performance, or receiving medical treatment, which represents core services for

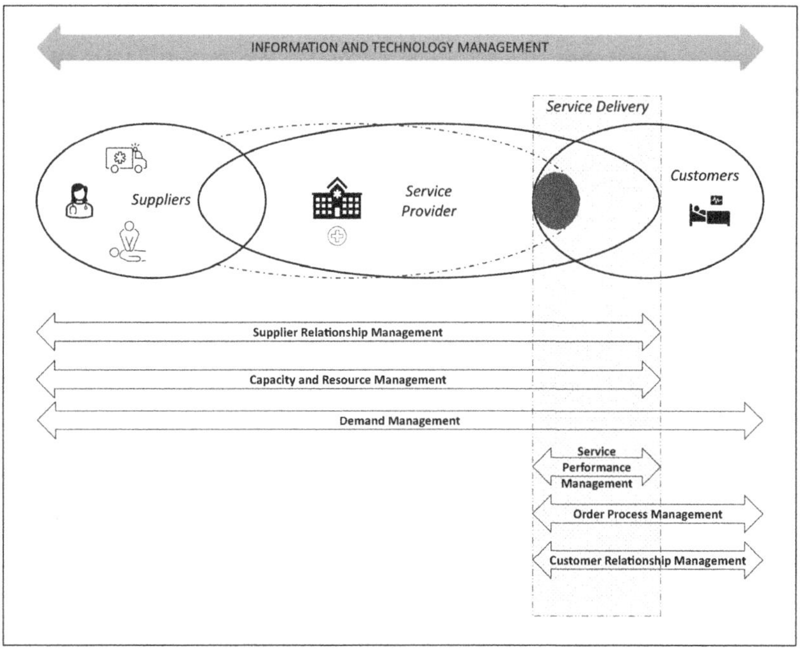

Fig. 2.4 Service supply chain model *Source: Authors generated based on* Baltacioglu et al. (2007)

customers. However, to provide these core services, service providers may require various supporting services, such as the transportation of goods or catering.

The roles of core and supporting services are decisive in the service supply chain. The service flow in a service supply chain encompasses both the core service and supporting services, which are collectively perceived as the expected service by the customer. Supporting services may be produced either by suppliers or by the service provider itself (Baltacioglu et al., 2007). It should also be noted that in a manufacturing-oriented supply chain, the focal flow is the material flow. In contrast, in a service supply chain context, supply chain management should start by focusing on the service as the main flow. Then, the materials and information flows must be aligned with the flow of service processes.

The successful delivery of services necessitates the seamless integration of “tangible objects”, such as materials, finished goods, machines, and equipment. According to Baltacioglu et al. (2007), tangible objects, referred to as “resources”, are fundamental to the effective performance of services. In addition to physical resources, additional elements such as the labour force, financial capital, and outsourced services from other firms play crucial roles in supporting service delivery.

In service supply chains, the processes involve transforming these resources into both core and supporting services. Each entity within the supply chain, including its subunits, must ensure the efficient execution and realisation of these processes. Furthermore, the management of information flow must be synchronised with the flow of services and materials to maintain efficiency and effectiveness. In the end, the value for the customer can only be created if all these flows and processes can be managed properly. To clarify this, we borrow the example given by Christopher (2023, p.234):

> *“…two different airlines might fly you from London Heathrow to JFK Airport in New York and get you there on time – the outcome is the same. However, the way the outcome is delivered is the real means of differentiation, particularly when it’s a service. Thus, in the case of competing airlines, the competitive differentials could be the booking system, the check-in process, employee attitude, and so on. The means by which a service is delivered is through the supply chain processes that are employed.”*

In this context, the effective management of service supply chains involves several key activities (Baltacioglu et al., 2007; Ellram et al., 2004), such as demand management, capacity and resource management, customer relationship management (CRM), supplier relationship management (SRM), order process management, service performance management, and information and technology management (Fig. 2.4). By focusing on these critical activities, organisations can significantly enhance the efficiency and effectiveness of their service supply chains, leading to improved service delivery and higher customer satisfaction. Therefore, understanding and implementing these principles is vital for businesses aiming to thrive in today's complex and dynamic global market. Each of these activities has a potential impact on creating value throughout the service delivery process and must be carefully managed by considering the dynamics of the market.

2.4 Challenges of Service Supply Chain Members During Disruptions

In the context of the dynamic global marketplace, it is important to emphasise that "service" plays a focal role in establishing a competitive advantage for every member of the supply chain. This is because service is part of every business, since the use of human effort and skills in transforming the material into a finished product or even managing all the organisation's resources to achieve the company's aim until consumers get what is demanded.

Certain industries are more vulnerable to these risks and consequent disruptions than others are (Berg et al., 2020; ILO, 2020), but it is clear that the service industry has been significantly impacted in recent years (Belhadi et al., 2021). The unique characteristics of service supply chains, such as the dependence on both service providers and consumers, as well as the intangible and perishable nature of services (Baltacioglu et al., 2007), pose distinct challenges for service supply chain (SSC) members. Unprecedented disruptions, such as the COVID-19 outbreak, have shown that SSCs face uncertainties, disturbances, and various risks on both the supply and demand sides (Belhadi et al., 2021), including transportation failures, supply shortages, and demand fluctuations (Ali et al., 2022; Ivanov & Dolgui, 2020; Sharma et al., 2020). Identifying these risks and developing effective mitigation strategies are relevant from both theoretical and practical perspectives, especially in response to such disruptions (Belhadi et al., 2021). Despite growing awareness in manufacturing-oriented business networks regarding the identification of risk mitigation strategies, the same level of attention has not been given to SSC settings.

Additionally, while there is scholarly interest in supply chain risk management in the service context, especially post-COVID-19 (e.g., Hohenstein, 2022; Belhadi et al., 2021; Ajmal et al., 2023), specific attention has not been given to risks and mitigation strategies in service supply chains across various sectors. In parallel, supply chain risk management and resilience strategies and practices in the context of services are not yet well developed. Therefore, our objective is to delve into these issues by considering different types of service businesses, such as tourism, healthcare, education, logistics, and professional services, in the context of service procurement and resilience.

To fully appreciate the criticality of service supply chain process management and its relevance to resilience, which is discussed in detail in Chapter 4, we reflect on different examples. For this purpose, Crandall et al., (2015, p.234) provide an interesting service example as follows:

> *"...It is apparent in most societies that there is a generally accepted flow of students within the formal education system. The process begins at kindergarten, and students progress to elementary school, junior high school (sometimes called middle school in certain areas), high school, college, and postgraduate school. After school is completed, the student moves to an employer and hopefully becomes an educated citizen in society. In each stage, the output from the previous stage becomes the input to the next stage, where it is transformed into another output to be passed on to the next stage in the supply chain. However, most of us do not think of the need to closely connect the stages of this supply chain to make it more effective. If we did, there would be greater collaboration among the different entities."*

As academics, we agree with the above example and believe that applying service supply chain principles to different aspects of human life can improve the entire educational journey as well as the skills and knowledge development processes in organisations. We will revisit these ideas in Chapters 5 and 6.

References

Ajmal, M. M., Khan, M., Shad, M. K., AlKatheeri, H., & Jabeen, F. (2023). Empirical examination of societal, financial and technology-related challenges amid COVID-19 in service supply chains: Evidence from emerging market. *The International Journal of Logistics Management, 34*(4), 994–1019.

Ali, I., Arslan, A., Chowdhury, M., Khan, Z., & Tarba, S. Y. (2022). Reimagining global food value chains through effective resilience to COVID-19 shocks and similar future events: A dynamic capability perspective. *Journal of Business Research, 141*, 1–12.

Allen, S., & Chandrashekar, A. (2000). Outsourcing services: The contract is just the beginning. *Business Horizons, 43*(2), 25–34.

Arlbjørn, J. S., Freytag, P. V., & Haas, H. (2011). Service supply chain management: A survey of lean application in the municipal sector. *International Journal of Physical Distribution & Logistics Management, 41*(3), 277–295.

Baines, T., & Lightfoot, H. W. (2013). Servitization of the manufacturing firm: Exploring the operations practices and technologies that deliver advanced services. *International Journal of Operations & Production Management, 34*(1), 2–35.

Balouei Jamkhaneh, H., Shahin, R., & Shahin, A. (2023). Assessing sustainable tourism development through service supply chain process maturity and service quality model. *International Journal of Productivity and Performance Management, 72*(7), 2046–2068.

Baltacioglu, T., Ada, E., Kaplan, M. D., Yurt, O., & Kaplan, Y. C. (2007). A new framework for services supply chains. *The Service Industries Journal, 27*(2), 105–124.

Belhadi, A., Kamble, S., Jabbour, C. J. C., Gunasekaran, A., Ndubisi, N. O., & Venkatesh, M. (2021). Manufacturing and service supply chain resilience to the COVID-19 outbreak: Lessons learned from the automobile and airline industries. *Technological Forecasting and Social Change, 163*, 120447.

Berg, L., Haug, L., Hedrich, S., & Magnus, K. H. (2020). Time for change: How to use the crisis to make fashion sourcing more agile and sustainable. *McKinsey & Company.* Retrieved from: https://www.mckinsey.com/industries/retail/our-insights/time-for-change-how-to-use-the-crisis-to-make-fashion-sourcing-more-agile-and-sustainable. (Last accessed: 23.06.2024)

Bruhn, M., & Georgi, D. (2006). *Services marketing: Managing the service value chain.* Prentice Hall.

Christopher, M. L. (1992). *Logistics and supply chain management.* Pitman Publishing.

Christopher, M. (2023). *Logistics and supply chain management* (6th ed.). Pearson International Content.
Christopher, M., & Holweg, M. (2011). Supply Chain 2.0": Managing supply chains in the era of turbulence. *International Journal of Physical Distribution & Logistics Management, 41*(1), 63–82.
Christopher, M., Mena, C., Khan, O., & Yurt, O. (2011). Approaches to managing global sourcing risk. *Supply Chain Management: An International Journal, 16*(2), 67–81.
Cook, J. S., DeBree, K., & Feroleto, A. (2002). From raw materials to customers: Supply chain management in the service industry. *SAM Advanced Management Journal, 66*(4), 14–21.
Craighead, C. W., Blackhurst, J., Rungtusanatham, M. J., & Handfield, R. B. (2007). The severity of supply chain disruptions: Design characteristics and mitigation capabilities. *Decision Sciences, 38*(1), 131–156.
Crandall, R. E., Crandall, W. R., & Chen, C. C. (2015). *Principles of supply chain management* (2nd ed.). CRC Press.
Crawford, J., & Jabbour, M. (2024). The relationship between enterprise risk management and managerial judgement in decision-making: A systematic literature review. *International Journal of Management Reviews, 26*, 110–136.
Ellram, L. M., Tate, W., & Billington, C. (2004). Understanding and managing the services supply chain. *The Journal of Supply Chain Management, 40*(4), 17–32.
Fitzsimmons, J. A., & Fitzsimmons, M. J. (2006). *Service management: Operations, strategy, and information technology* (5th ed.). McGraw Hill.
Giannakis, M. (2011). Conceptualizing and managing service supply chains. *The Service Industries Journal, 31*(11), 1809–1823.
Grönroos, C. (1990). *Service management and marketing: Managing the moment of truth in service competition*. Lexington Books.
Gurbuz, M. C., Yurt, O., Ozdemir, S., Sena, V., & Yu, W. (2023). Global supply chains risks and COVID-19: Supply chain structure as a mitigating strategy for small and medium-sized enterprises. *Journal of Business Research, 155*, 113407.
Hohenstein, N. O. (2022). Supply chain risk management in the COVID-19 pandemic: Strategies and empirical lessons for improving global logistics service providers' performance. *The International Journal of Logistics Management, 33*(4), 1336–1365.
Hutton, G. (2024). Business statistics-Research briefings, House of Commons Library. Available at: https://researchbriefings.files.parliament.uk/documents/SN06152/SN06152.pdf (Last accessed: 20.06.2024).

International Labour Organization (ILO). (2020). COVID-19 and the textiles, clothing, leather and footwear industries. Retrieved from: https://www.ilo.org/wcmsp5/groups/public/-ed_dialogue/-sector/documents/briefingnote/wcms_741344.pdf (Last accessed: 20.06.2024).

Ivanov, D., & Dolgui, A. (2020). Viability of intertwined supply networks: Extending the supply chain resilience angles towards survivability. A position paper motivated by COVID-19 outbreak. *International Journal of Production Research, 58*(10), 2904–2915.

Johnston, R., & Clark, G. (2005). *Service operations management: improving service delivery* (3rd ed.). Pearson Education.

Jüttner, U., Peck, H., & Christopher, M. (2003). Supply chain risk management: Outlining an agenda for future research. *International Journal of Logistics: Research and Applications, 6*(4), 197–210.

Kathawala, Y., & Abdou, K. (2003). Supply chain evaluation in the service industry: A framework development compared to manufacturing. *Managerial Auditing Journal, 18*(2), 140–149.

Lambert, D., Stock, J. R., & Ellram, L. M. (1998). *Fundamentals of logistics management*. Irwin/McGraw-Hill.

Lusch, R. F. (2011). Reframing supply chain management: A service-dominant logic perspective. *Journal of Supply Chain Management, 47*, 14–18.

Mentzer, J. T., DeWitt, W., Keebler, J. S., Min, S., Nix, N. W., Smith, C. D., & Zacharia, Z. G. (2001). Defining supply chain management. *Journal of Business Logistics, 22*(2), 1–25.

Naeini, S. A. B., & Badri, A. (2024). Identification and categorization of hazards in the mining industry: A systematic review of the literature. *International Review of Applied Sciences and Engineering, 15*(1), 1–19.

Neely, A., Benedittini, O., & Visnjic, I. (2011). The servitization of manufacturing: Further evidence. Paper presented at the *18th European Operations Management Association Conference*, Cambridge. Retrieved from https://cambridgeservicealliance.eng.cam.ac.uk/resources/Downloads/berlinserviceskeynote.pdf (Last accessed: 02.03.2020).

Nie, W., & Kellogg, D. L. (1999). How professors of operations management view service operations? *Production and Operations Management, 8*(3), 339–355.

Pereira, C. R., Christopher, M., & Silva, A. L. (2014). Achieving supply chain resilience: The role of procurement. *Supply Chain Management: An International Journal, 19*(5/6), 626–642.

Rapaccini, M., & Visintin, F. (2015). Devising hybrid solutions: An exploratory framework. *Production Planning & Control, 26*(8), 654–672.

Sampson, S. E. (2000). Customer-supplier duality and bidirectional supply chains in service organizations. *International Journal of Service Industry Management, 11*(4), 348–364.

Sampson, S. E., & Spring, M. (2012a). Customer roles in service supply chains and opportunities for innovation. *Journal of Supply Chain Management, 48*(4), 30–50.

Sampson, S. E., & Spring, M. (2012b). Service supply chains: Introducing the special topic forum. *Journal of Supply Chain Management, 48*(4), 3–7.

Schmenner, R. W. (2009). Manufacturing, service, and their integration: Some history and theory. *International Journal of Operations & Production Management, 29*(5), 431–443.

Sharma, A., Adhikary, A., & Borah, S. B. (2020). COVID-19's impact on supply chain decisions: Strategic insights from NASDAQ 100 firms using Twitter data. *Journal of Business Research, 117*, 443–449.

Statista. (2024). Global gross domestic product (GDP) at current prices from 1985 to 2028. Retrieved from https://www.statista.com/statistics/268750/global-gross-domestic-product-gdp/ (Last accessed: 10.05.2024)

Tukker, A. (2004). Eight types of product-service system: Eight ways to sustainability? Experiences from SusProNet. *Business Strategy and the Environment, 13*(4), 246–260.

Tuli, K. R., Kohli, A. K., & Bharadwaj, S. G. (2007). Rethinking customer solutions: From product bundles to relational processes. *Journal of Marketing, 71*(3), 1–17.

Vargo, S. L., & Lusch, R. F. (2004). Evolving to a new dominant logic for marketing. *Journal of Marketing, 68*(1), 1–17.

Walletzký, L., Carrubbo, L., Badr, N. G., Dragoicea, M., Toli, A. M., & Badawi, S. (2023). Reconfiguring the service system for resilience: Lessons learned in the higher education context. *Journal of Business & Industrial Marketing., 39*, 1144–1161.

Wang, Y., Wallace, S. V., Shen, B., & Choi, T. (2015). Service supply chain management: A review of operational models. *European Journal of Operational Research, 247*(3), 685–698.

Wirtz, J., & Lovelock, C. (2018). *Essential of services marketing* (3rd ed.). Pearson Education.

World Economic Forum. (2024). The global risks report: Insight report, 19th edition. Retrieved from https://www3.weforum.org/docs/WEF_The_Global_Risks_Report_2024.pdf (Last accessed: 04.05.2024)

World Trade Organization (WTO) & The World Bank. (2024). Trade in services for development: Fostering sustainable growth and economic diversification.

Retrieved from https://www.wto.org/english/res_e/booksp_e/trade_in_services_and_development_e.pdf (Last accessed: 04.05.2024)
Zeithaml, V. A., Bitner, M. J., & Gremler, D. D. (2006). *Services marketing: Integrating Customer Focus Across the Firm* (4th ed.). London: McGraw-Hill.
Zhang, R., & Chen, H. (2015). A review of service supply chain and future prospects. *Journal of Service Science and Management, 8*(4), 485–495.

CHAPTER 3

The Role of Procurement in Service Supply Chains

Abstract In this chapter, the concept of procurement is first introduced, covering its evolution and terminology differences. It then emphasises the main areas of managing resources, the responsibilities of a procurement team, and how it acts as a boundary-spanning function. Considering the role of "humans" in procurement, the chapter highlights some skills and competencies. Additionally, it reflects on service supply chain professionals and the relation between service procurement and procurement in the service supply chain.

Keywords Procurement function · Skills and competencies · Service procurement

To better understand the role of procurement in service supply chains, it is vital to recognise the importance of effectively managing the flow of services within these supply chains. Additionally, emphasising the need to support the flow of materials and information is essential to highlight the required shift in mindset for supply chain professionals involved in service supply chains. In this chapter, we cover the origins of procurement as a business function and its main responsibilities, as well as how this function is perceived and operates in the service sector.

C. Pereira and Ö. Yurt, *Achieving Resilience in Service Supply Chains*, Palgrave Studies in Logistics and Supply Chain Management, https://doi.org/10.1007/978-3-031-68244-5_3

3.1 Procurement as a Business Function

To obtain a proper understanding of the procurement concept (from a manufacturing perspective), the immediate focus is often on the volume and cost of purchases, considering the influence it has in promoting cost savings since much of the product cost is directly linked to raw material expenses. However, as discussed in the previous chapter, procuring services carry further complexities due to their distinctive characteristics (e.g., perishability, intangibility, simultaneity, and heterogeneity). This idea will be further explored in Sect. 3.3 of this chapter. However, for now, let us have a deeper look at the basic concept of procurement and its origin.

Considering the contributions of the seminal works of Cousins et al. (2008) and Monckza et al. (2005), this function has evolved through four stages over the years.

Stage 1—Passive (early 1900).

In this stage, the function is commonly named purchasing and operates at the lowest contribution level for the organisation, lacking a strategic direction and merely reacting to requests from other departments. Therefore, the purchasing manager, if present, mainly addresses immediate supply problems and routine operations. The focus is primarily on efficiency and cost, and historically, the main goal has been to find suppliers that offer the lowest price and the highest availability. Nevertheless, at this stage, there is minimal communication between different departments, and the overall result is, therefore, a function with untapped potential, operating reactively and missing opportunities for more strategic and value-driven contributions to the organisation.

Stage 2—Independent (approximately 1920 to 1970).

The function adopts the latest purchasing techniques and tools, such as value analysis, information technology links, and supplier partnerships, in line with external market practices. However, at this stage, it may not immediately contribute to a competitive advantage, and benchmarking against competitors becomes imperative for survival in the marketplace. Despite still being centred on cost reduction and efficiency measures, it has gained recognition as a vital contributor to the organisation's profitability, albeit operating independently of the overall competitive strategy.

Stage 3—Supportive (approximately early 1970 to late 1990).

The function has now ascended to the "top division" within its market, achieving a status where they are broadly comparable with the best competitors. While they may not excel in every aspect, they maintain competitive parity. In this stage, it becomes inherently "supportive" of the firm's strategy, emphasising alignment when making decisions both in purchasing and across departments. Top management recognises the purchasing function as essential for business alignment and competitive strategy. At this stage, some organisations started to name this function procurement. This involves providing timely information to all departments about potential changes in the price and availability of materials, which could impact the firm's strategic goals. Moreover, it demonstrates proficiency in managing the flow of goods and information internally and externally, focusing on careful selection and continuous monitoring of suppliers.

Stage 4—Integrative (from 2000 onwards).

Procurement becomes a crucial part of the firm's competitive strategy at this stage. It looks at long-term plans, joins in strategic planning sessions, and takes steps to predict changes in supply markets. The main aim is to stay ahead of competitors, ready to seize opportunities, and prevent potential problems. The procurement plan is smoothly included in the overall organisational strategy, keeping open lines of communication with other parts of the business. Procurement is also actively involved in reshaping business processes, making the organisation work better and giving it a more decisive competitive edge.

Figure 3.1 outlines the key milestones in the evolution of the procurement function since the late 1850s. The function has changed dramatically from simply buying goods and services to overseeing an integrated set of management functions. In addition to advanced digital integration into procurement processes, it is now considered a proactive and strategic part of the organisation (Althabatah et al., 2023).

In terms of terminologies, several authors (e.g., Althabatah et al., 2023; Ellram & Carr, 1994; Sobhani et al., 2014) assert that procurement is an evolution of purchasing, now encompassing purchase processes and even supply management. However, both concepts are sometimes treated interchangeably in the literature. In addition, sourcing or supply management are other procurement-related terminologies. Monczka et al. (2005) describe this as the process of identifying, evaluating, selecting, managing, and developing suppliers to achieve better performance than competitors. Finally, purchasing and supply management (PSM) is also a widely known

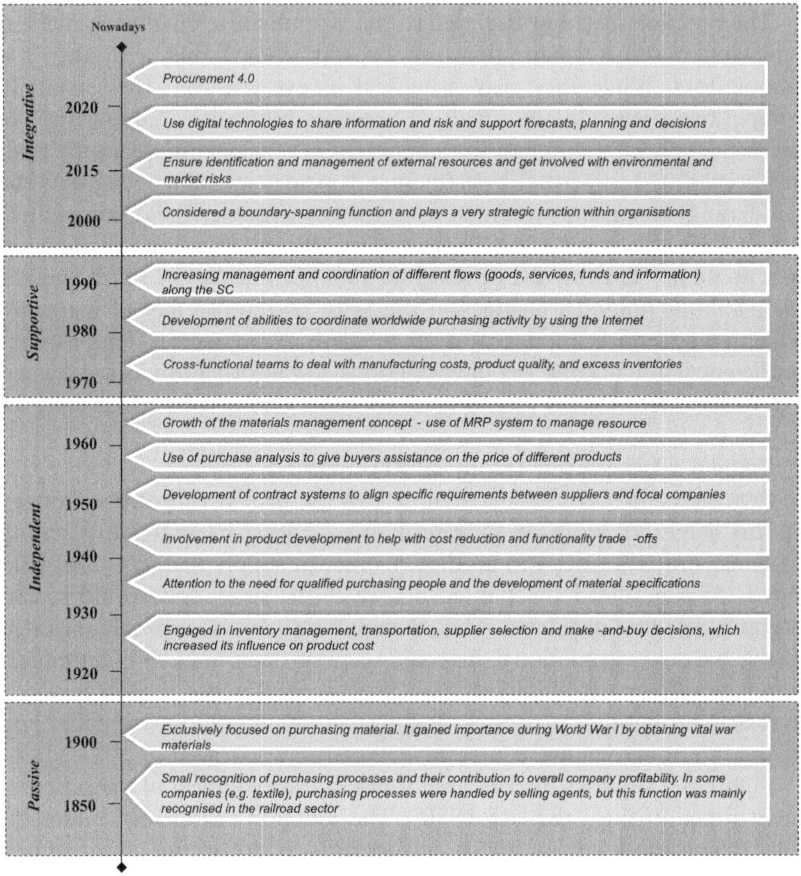

Fig. 3.1 The historical evolution of the procurement function *Source: Based on several sources, such as* Monczka et al. (2005), Cousins et al. (2008), Pereira et al. (2014), Bienhaus and Haddud (2018), Küffner et al. (2022) *and* Althabatah et al. (2023)

and discussed term for this function, and several studies have explored, discussed, and defined it at the same level of content and complexity as procurement (e.g., Pereira et al., 2020; Küffner et al., 2022).

The Chartered Institute of Purchasing and Supply (2024) officially outlines procurement as "*the business management function that ensures identification, sourcing, access and management of the external resources that an organisation needs or may need to fulfil its strategic objectives".* In essence, procurement is broadly described as any method of acquiring goods through purchasing, leasing, renting, or obtaining supplies or services from external suppliers. This concept covers all responsibilities that managers are expected to handle, such as identifying, sourcing, accessing, and managing resources outside the company. It also implies achieving the company's strategic goals to create significant business value and positively impact profits.

Ultimately, bringing to light the innovativeness and importance of procurement to today's business, Althabatah et al. (2023) introduce the concept of Procurement 4.0 (P4.0). This term is part of Industry 4.0 and establishes a network connecting all partners in the supply chain, allowing quick cooperation and coordination beyond organisational boundaries. Their study discussed how integrating e-procurement, big data analytics, IoT, additive manufacturing, blockchain, and AI can improve efficiency, transparency, collaboration, and decision-making in procurement processes. Nevertheless, they also emphasise the importance of carefully considering risks, challenges, and the human element when adopting these technologies.

In general, procurement is no longer seen as a static function in today's rapidly evolving business landscape. It is now a dynamic role that must navigate many uncertainties and disruptive events across supply chains. This evolution has elevated procurement to a pivotal position in ensuring business maintenance and survival, which is no longer perceived merely as a resource management function but as a strategic driver of value (Pereira, 2014, 2020). To do so, this function has key areas that should be well thought and managed, as will be discussed in the following section.

3.1.1 Key Areas Supporting Procurement

The following key areas support the development of strategies and approaches that align with the organisation's mission and vision (Monczka et al., 2005).

- ***Human Resources:*** *Knowledge and skills from* procurement professionals are key factors to consider when hiring staff or developing over the years. For instance, expertise in cost management analysis from external sources and consequent consistent decisions, experience and skills in communicating, fostering good relationships with suppliers, and knowledge of current digital technologies. Gaining access to the right skills will require a sound human resource strategy that includes the internal development of high-potential individuals and/or the recruitment of talent from other functional groups or companies with specific skills and competencies. This topic will be further discussed in Sect. 3.2.

- ***Organisational Structure or Hierarchy***: This is related to how organisations are internally structured and, therefore, how they maintain their formal system of communication, establish authority and delegate responsibilities, and coordinate and control processes. In this regard, cross-functional teams are usually developed to manage intra- and interorganisational processes. This topic will be further explained in Sect. 3.1.2
- ***Information Technology***: There are an increasing number of new technologies that involve synchronous or asynchronous information sharing, from traditional methods such as enterprise resource planning (ERP) and supplier relationship management (SRM) by using simple electronic data interchange (EDI) applications to new digital and advanced technologies, such as digital twins, blockchain, and the Internet of Things (IoT). As much as there is a need for procurement professionals to develop skills and competencies in current technologies (as previously highlighted and especially to support the new concept of Procurement 4.0), there is a need to consider the size, sector, and structure of the company, as well as its financial condition, to implement and make effective use of an array of currently available technologies. This is further discussed in the "release and receive purchase requirements" section in Sect. 3.1.3 and then in Chapters 5 and 6.
- ***Performance Measurement***: Although this is a very common term in business, several studies (e.g., Giannakis et al., 2020; Maestrini et al., 2018) have shown that companies still lack a common system for measuring supplier performance—a key component of supply chain effectiveness. Monitoring key performance indicators from the company's side as well as from the suppliers' side is important because it supports fact-based rather than subjective decision-making. This, therefore, plays a fundamental role in setting up targets and searching for continuous improvement. This topic is

also examined in Sect. 3.1.3 when considering the measurement of supplier performance.

3.1.2 Procurement as a Boundary-Spanning Function

As previously explained, procurement has become important due to ongoing changes in business and its involvement in various activities across the company. According to the Chartered Institute of Purchasing and Supply (2024), procurement activities may include market analysis, sourcing, negotiation, contracting, and supplier relationship management for goods, works, and services, encompassing acquisitions from external suppliers and those from in-house providers. Thus, it covers the entire procurement cycle, from identifying organisational needs to the conclusion of a service contract or the end of a product's useful life.

In addition to these activities, supplier development is considered an extra initiative to enhance suppliers' operations, quality, and performance. This, in turn, will positively impact the organisation (Monczka et al., 2005; Sobhani et al., 2014). Risk management is another key activity that cannot be missed when dealing with a variety of internal and external resources. Understanding how procurement professionals identify, monitor, and manage potential risks (mainly on the supply side) involves understanding what factors could negatively impact inbound supply and the financial consequences of these events on the organisation's performance. Therefore, procurement's perspective on supply-side risk sources and the likelihood of supply disruption is usually shaped by the availability of the organisation's data recorded and its lessons learned from an array of events. The main reason is that not all risks are similar, and managing supply disruptions should not follow a one-size-fits-all approach. Therefore, identifying different risk sources is essential for developing a tailored strategy to reduce the occurrence of supply disruptions (Zsidisin et al., 2000).

Overall, there are four key principles that procurement should be aware of to develop successful strategies:

- Align the procurement goals with the organisation's strategy,
- Develop specific knowledge and skills for the procurement professionals,
- Establish close and trustful relationships with key suppliers,

- Promote effective intra- and interorganisational relationships.

Adhering to these principles can make procurement a boundary-spanning function that effectively bridges the gap between internal and external organisations (Fig. 3.2).

Now, looking at the synergy of the flows, information across functional areas undergoes an internal dynamic process until *procurement* initiates orders with suppliers. With collaborative efforts between *product development* and *marketing* to conceptualise market demands, information flows through procurement to align purchasing strategies with organisational goals. Subsequently, *production* receives specific details on material requirements, while *quality assurance* ensures adherence to set standards. *Sales* and *marketing* teams stay informed about product availability and specifications, contributing to effective customer communication. Simultaneously, *accounting and finance* track financial aspects related to procurement decisions. These interconnected flows ensure synchronised and efficient operations until procurement places orders with suppliers, solidifying the integration of diverse functional areas. Nevertheless, this is not possible if the organisation does not support communication through technologies, flexible structures, or training skills and knowledge development (Küffner et al., 2022).

Similar to internal relationships, procurement should be heavily engaged in the upstream activities of the supply chain, enhancing processes for greater effectiveness, efficiency, and sustainability (Schoenherr et al., 2012). As mentioned above, it holds responsibility for selecting and managing multiple sources as well as their relationships, determining product or service costs, setting delivery deadlines, and ensuring product quality. Hence, each decision this function makes has varied impacts on business performance (Althabatah et al., 2023; Pereira et al., 2020). With its direct connection to the enterprise's external part, procurement is also responsible for mitigating risks and overcoming environmental or supply-side problems. To do so, strong relationships with different tier suppliers (e.g., second and third tiers) need to be developed, promoting trust, collaboration, and information sharing, thereby ensuring satisfaction on both sides of the chain (Pereira, 2014).

In conclusion, procurement plays a pivotal intermediary role between external suppliers and internal organisational customers in creating and delivering value to external customers. It pays attention to both sides of the enterprise to find proper and reasonable solutions. Moreover, by

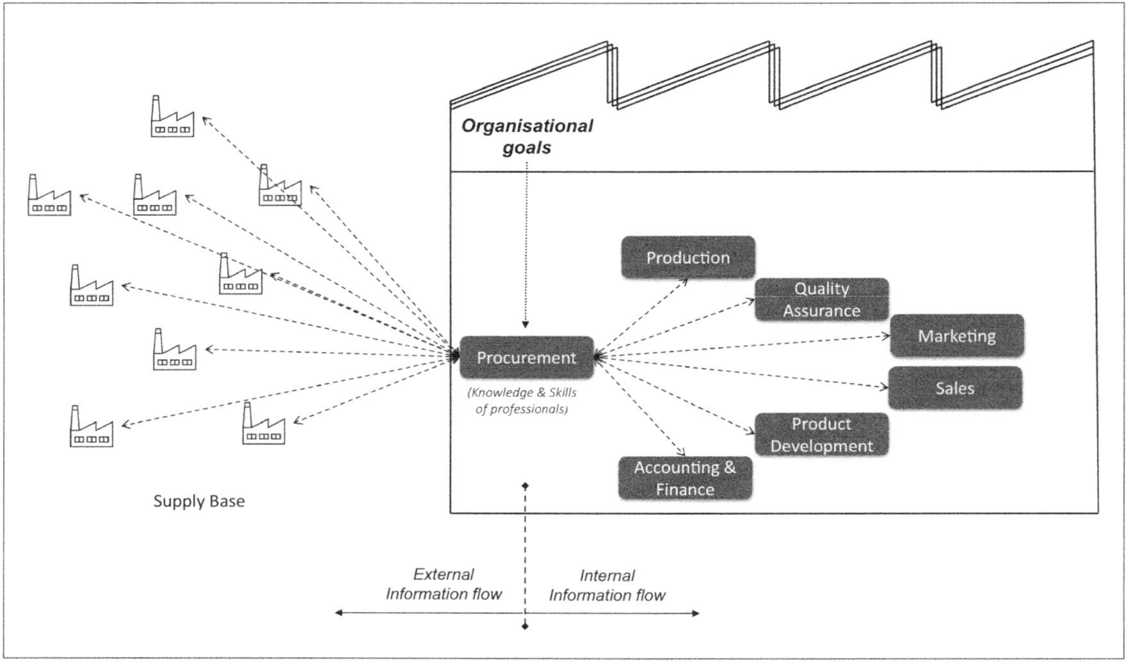

Fig. 3.2 Procurement as a boundary-spanning function *Source: Adapted from* Pereira et al. (2014)

synchronising the flows of goods and information between the buyer and supplier, it has the ability to communicate changes in market demand to suppliers, enabling the company and its supply chain to be responsive.

Finally, from the supply chain management perspective, procurement is considered a critical part of the supply chain since it directly affects the overall performance of the whole supply chain (Althabatah et al., 2023) since it integrates external resources and blends them with in-house resources to create new and competitive capabilities for the organisation (Schmelzle & Tate, 2022; Schmelzle et al., 2023). Therefore, we wanted to highlight the criticality of procurement in choosing the right resources and making assertive decisions to support organisations in dealing with several disruptive events. This view provides the basis for our further reflections on Chapters 5 and 6.

3.1.3 Main Responsibilities of Procurement

In this section, we will detail the main decision areas that are rightfully part of procurement daily activities in most organisations (Monczka et al., 2005; Wisner & Stanley, 2008).

- ***Identifying User Needs for Products or Services***: Engaging with end-users and key stakeholders helps in understanding the exact specifications and features needed. In some organisations, procurement managers can spend much more time upfront evaluating potential and discussing product or service specifications with internal functional areas to be precise in searching for suitable sourcing suppliers. This collaborative approach ensures that the selected suppliers meet the organisation's specific needs and expectations.
- ***Evaluate Potential Suppliers***: Conducting thorough assessments of potential suppliers involves not only identifying a supplier that produces what is expected but also scrutinising its financial stability, production capabilities, quality control measures, and previous performance. This evaluation (which may use a range of multiple criteria decision-making methods) helps identify reliable partners who align with the organisation's objectives. For some items, companies may maintain a list of "preferred suppliers" (who have demonstrated capability through past performance checks) who receive the first opportunity for a new order. This helps to reduce the time and resources required to evaluate and select suppliers.

- o ***Bidding, Negotiation, and Supplier Selection***: The bidding and negotiation process allows procurement professionals to secure competitive pricing and favourable contract terms. Bidding processes are commonly conducted when the product or service does not add high value so that the lowest bidder will receive the purchase contract. However, in regard to more strategic and value-adding items, negotiations are conducted where other assessing variables are involved. This phase is critical for selecting suppliers that offer the best value for the organisation while meeting quality and delivery requirements.
- o ***Approval for Purchasing***: Procurement professionals must obtain approval from relevant stakeholders or management (e.g., shareholders or the company's CEO) before finalising purchases. This ensures transparency, compliance with budgetary constraints, and alignment with overall business strategies.
- o ***Release and Receive Purchase Requirements***: Procurement professionals release purchase orders to selected suppliers once purchases are approved. Effective communication during this phase is essential for conveying precise requirements, delivery schedules, and other pertinent details. Upon delivery, procurement ensures that all items received meet the specified standards. To do so, procurement professionals leverage modern technologies to streamline the process of releasing purchase orders and managing subsequent communication with suppliers. Procurement software, such as enterprise resource planning (ERP) systems and e-procurement platforms, facilitates automated purchase order generation and electronic transmission to selected suppliers. These platforms often include features for real-time tracking, enabling procurement teams to monitor the status of orders and receive timely updates on delivery schedules. Additionally, electronic data interchange (EDI) and cloud-based collaboration tools enhance communication efficiency by providing a centralised platform for sharing precise requirements, specifications, and any relevant documentation. Upon delivery, technologies such as barcode scanning and RFID systems are employed to verify that all items align with the specified standards, ensuring accuracy and reducing the risk of errors in the procurement process. This technology integration improves the speed and accuracy of purchase order management (supporting just-in-time production for some

companies) and enhances transparency and collaboration throughout the supply chain.

- o ***Measure of Supplier Performance***: Key performance indicators (KPIs) help quantify and measure supplier performance. Metrics such as on-time delivery, quality of goods or services, and responsiveness contribute to assessing and improving supplier relationships. Periodic evaluations provide insights into supplier strengths and areas for improvement. Feedback sessions (which can occur in different periods, depending on the company's risk assessment and the supplier's performance) with suppliers may foster continuous improvement and help promptly address any issues. Monitoring supplier performance also involves identifying and mitigating potential risks. This proactive approach ensures that the organisation can respond effectively to challenges and maintain a resilient supply chain.
- o ***Supply Management***: This involves the strategic oversight of the supply base, where procurement professionals actively engage and collaborate directly with selected suppliers. This goes beyond mere transactional interactions, fostering more profound and collaborative relationships with specifically chosen suppliers. In this dynamic process, procurement professionals aim not only to ensure a smooth flow of goods and services but also to contribute to supplier development. By actively participating in the growth and improvement of key suppliers, organisations can enhance their supply chain's overall efficiency, innovation, and reliability. This approach transcends traditional procurement practices, emphasising the importance of cultivating mutually beneficial, sustainable partnerships conducive to continuous improvement in product or service delivery and supplier capabilities. One of the worldwide strategic procurement tools used in supply management is the Kraljic matrix. This finding supports the analysis and management of a company's purchasing portfolio by helping companies categorise their products or services based on two key dimensions: supply risk and profit impact. By plotting items on these dimensions, procurement professionals can develop specific strategies for each category, tailoring their approach to maximise efficiency and mitigate risks (Fig. 3.3).

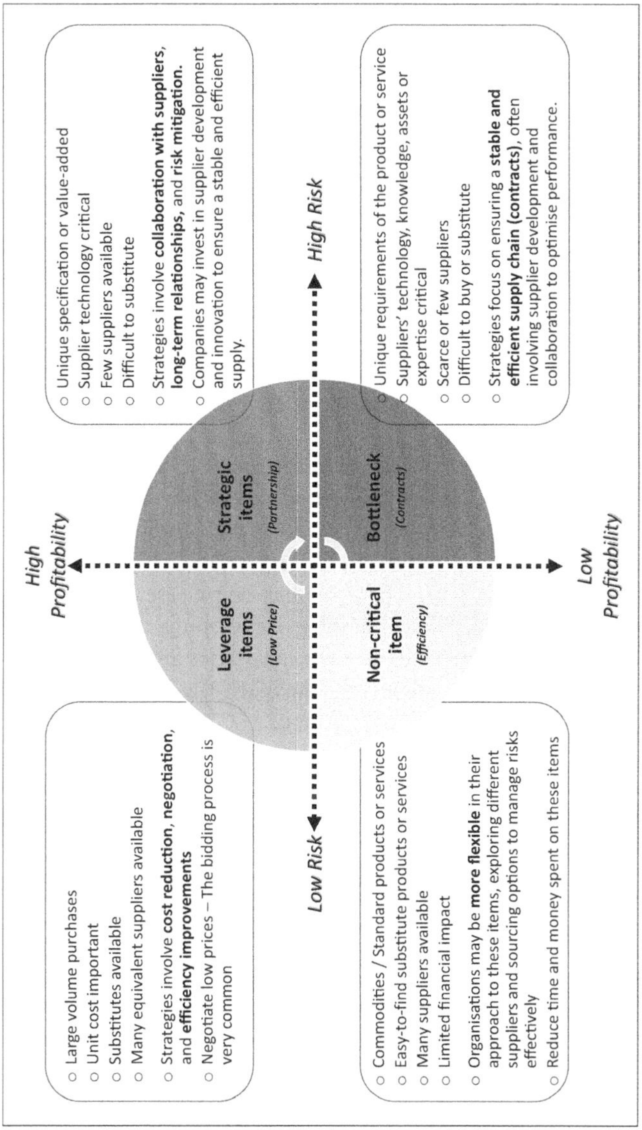

Fig. 3.3 Kraljic matrix for strategic procurement *Source: Adapted from* Kraljic (1983)

3.2 Skills and Competencies of Procurement Professionals

To address these dynamic changes and various disruptive events (following examples in Chapter 2), procurement professionals play an essential role in managing the complex interface between organisations and their stakeholders to maximise the value and efficiency of operations. To achieve this goal, an increasingly comprehensive set of skills and competencies needs to be developed and implemented (Beske-Janssen et al., 2023). As previously stated, this is critical for procurement managers, given their need to think holistically about the business (internally and externally). This could be easily linked to what Christopher (2023) mentioned as a "T-shaped skills profile" in supply chains, where managers have specific expertise with in-depth knowledge and capability, in addition to a significant understanding of the other key functional areas.

Previous research by scholars, such as Mangan and Christopher (2005), Prajogo and Sohal (2013), Beske-Janssen et al. (2023), and Changalima and Mdee (2023), has delved into the skills and competencies essential for procurement and supply chain management professionals in the twenty-first century (Table 3.1). These studies emphasise the significance of professionals being aware of and actively developing these competencies. We understand that these skills and competencies are fundamental for procurement professionals to effectively navigate the challenges around the current dynamic and volatile environment.

Additionally, by combining the above skills and competencies, procurement professionals can increase their ability to identify alternative sources, develop robust supplier relationships, and implement agile strategies to mitigate the impact of disruptions. For instance, by developing the ability to anticipate risks and think strategically about acknowledging available resources, procurement managers will be able to address immediate problems without having ways to mitigate them in the future. This, therefore, serves as a strategic shield, enabling organisations to navigate uncertainties and emerge more vital in an ever-changing business environment.

Finally, we believe that HEIs, where business schools are embedded, have a role in responding to these trends and providing the future generation of procurement professionals with an appropriate portfolio of competencies. Recent research has begun to explore these new competencies and has called for more related research (Beske-Janssen et al., 2023;

Table 3.1 Skills and competencies of procurement professionals *Source: Adapted from* Mangan and Christopher (2005), Prajogo and Sohal (2013), Beske-Janssen et al. (2023), *and* Changalima and Mdee (2023)

Skills and competences	*Description*
Strategic Thinking	Ability to align procurement strategies with overall business objectives, foresee potential challenges and proactively plan for uncertainties
Risk Management	Proficiency in identifying, assessing, and mitigating risks associated with the supply chain, including geopolitical, economic, and operational risks
Negotiation Skills	Strong negotiation skills are crucial for securing favourable terms with suppliers, managing costs, and navigating complex contractual arrangements
Supplier Relationship Management (SRM)	Building and maintaining solid relationships with suppliers to ensure a reliable and collaborative supply chain network
Technology Proficiency	Familiarity with procurement technologies, such as e-procurement systems and supply chain management software, to enhance efficiency and visibility
Data Analytics	Utilising data analytics tools to gather and analyse information for informed decision-making, forecasting, and identifying opportunities for cost savings
Communication Skills	Clear and effective communication is essential for collaborating with internal teams, suppliers, and other stakeholders, especially in times of uncertainty
Problem-Solving	Strong problem-solving skills to address unforeseen challenges and find innovative solutions to maintain the flow of goods and services
Continuous Learning	Keeping abreast of industry trends, emerging technologies, and best practices through continuous learning and professional development
Global Awareness	Understanding global market trends, international trade regulations, and geopolitical dynamics impacting the supply chain

(continued)

Table 3.1 (continued)

Skills and competences	*Description*
Ethical and sustainable Procurement	Adherence to ethical standards and the ability to ensure that procurement practices align with corporate social responsibility and sustainability goals
Regulatory Compliance	Staying informed about and ensuring compliance with relevant laws, regulations, and industry standards

Schulze et al., 2019). In this sense, we will return to these skills and competencies in Chapter 6 to provide insights into how they can support the development of resilience in the service supply chain.

3.3 Service Procurement and Procurement in the Service Supply Chain

It is essential to clarify the difference between service procurement and procurement in the service supply chain, as they are two related but distinct concepts. By service procurement, we mean acquiring services from external suppliers or providers relevant to both (traditional) manufacturing-oriented supply chains and service supply chains (Fitzsimmons & Fitzsimmons, 2006). On the other hand, procurement in the service supply chain refers to the broader process of purchasing goods, services, and resources necessary to support the delivery of services in a service-oriented supply chain (in which service is the primary flow, whereas information and material are supportive flows) (Ellram et al., 2004). Therefore, procurement in the service supply chain encompasses the end-to-end activities involved in sourcing and managing inputs that enable the provision of services. Hence, understanding service procurement is the first step in understanding service supply chains. Effective service supply chain management is achieved when several service procurement activities and transactions are seamlessly integrated and managed.

In supply chain management, services include a wide range of activities, from supplementary services (such as office cleaning and corporate catering) to core operating services (such as quality assurance and supply chain management)—a concept primarily explained in Fig. 2.3 in

Chapter 2. Additionally, strategic services (such as market research and IT infrastructure development) are critical in determining a company's long-term success. The procurement role also includes acquiring critical services that, while not visible in day-to-day operations, have a substantial impact on workforce well-being, such as employee wellness programmes and professional development training.

Purchasing services tends to be more difficult than purchasing tangible goods because measuring the quality of services rather than goods is more complicated. Additionally, services are frequently packaged in extended-term contracts, which require less formal methods for measuring the performance of suppliers (Crandall et al., 2015). The root causes of these differences are the distinctive characteristics of services (e.g., perishability, intangibility, simultaneity, and heterogeneity) discussed in Chapter 2.

Considering the differences between physical goods and services and the distinguishing characteristics between the procurement of goods and services, companies need to put extra effort into service purchasing by effectively dedicating more resources to service procurement. According to Ellram et al. (2007), developing the required organisational capabilities in service procurement is the key, as it is the next frontier for improving the supply chain and organisational performance. We build on this view and propose that the skills and capabilities of procurement and supply chain professionals play a vital role in overall chain performance, given the particular importance of the service sector for the UK and developed economies in general. We will continue this reflection in the following section.

3.4 Supply Chain Professionals in the Service Industry

Especially after the impacts of COVID-19, supply chain professionals have found themselves in a more challenging position, as they need to manage increasingly complex and dynamic supply chain processes to sustain running supply chain operations (Belhadi et al., 2021). As we discussed, the literature acknowledges the importance of specific skills and competencies for supply chain professionals (Jordan & Bak, 2016); however, in practice, there is a shortage of talented supply chain professionals (e.g., Ellinger & Ellinger, 2014; Jordan & Bak, 2016). Part of this shortage may be explained by the fact that while skills and competencies for supply chain professionals are well identified in the literature, they are mainly focused on the manufacturing industry (Lorentz et al., 2013). This is problematic considering the development of the service industry and its impact on today's economy. Hence, exploring distinctive skills and relevant competencies for professionals in service supply chains is critical.

Moreover, due to the diversity and complexity of services, service procurement requires the involvement of many people from different functions, which critically requires cross-functional working teams. For instance, when a procurement professional needs to manage the purchase of logistics services, they should make a wide range of critical decisions (e.g., evaluating cost effectiveness, assessing service provider reliability, determining the scalability of services, and ensuring compliance with regulatory requirements) at the same time. Finding the best alternative service providers requires paying particular attention to service characteristics, personnel, and required service quality.

In Chapter 6, we discuss the importance of supply chain professionals' communication, collaboration, and teamwork skills, not only with individuals within their organisations but also with other supply chain members.

References

Althabatah, A., Yaqot, M., Menezes, B., & Kerbache, L. (2023). Transformative procurement trends: Integrating Industry 4.0 technologies for enhanced procurement processes. *Logistics, 7*(3), 63.

Belhadi, A., Kamble, S., Jabbour, C. J. C., Gunasekaran, A., Ndubisi, N. O., & Venkatesh, M. (2021). Manufacturing and service supply chain resilience to the COVID-19 outbreak: Lessons learned from the automobile and airline industries. *Technological Forecasting and Social Change, 163*, 120447.

Beske-Janssen, P., Johnsen, T., Constant, F., & Wieland, A. (2023). New competencies enhancing procurement's contribution to innovation and sustainability. *Journal of Purchasing and Supply Management, 29*(3), 100847.

Bienhaus, F., & Haddud, A. (2018). Procurement 4.0: factors influencing the digitisation of procurement and supply chains. *Business Process Management Journal, 24*(4), 965–984.

Changalima, I. A., & Mdee, A. E. (2023). Procurement skills and procurement performance in public organizations: The mediating role of procurement planning. *Cogent Business & Management, 10*(1), 2163562.

Chartered Institute of Purchasing & Supply (CIPS). (2024). What is procurement? Explore what procurement is, the role it plays and how a career in procurement can benefit you. Retrieved from https://www.cips.org/intelligence-hub/procurement/what-is-procurement (Last accessed: 13.03.2024 March 2024).

Christopher, M. (2023). *Logistics & supply chain management* (6th ed.). NJ: FT Publishing International.

Cousins, P., Lamming, R., Lawson, B., & Squire, B. (2008). *Strategic supply management: Principles, theories and practice*. Pearson Education.

Crandall, R. E., Crandall, W. R., & Chen, C. C. (2015). *Principles of supply chain management* (2nd ed.). CRC Press.

Ellinger, E. A., & Ellinger, D. A. (2014). Leveraging human resource development expertise to improve supply chain managers' skills and competencies. *European Journal of Training and Development, 38*(1/2), 118–135.

Ellram, L. M., & Carr, A. (1994). Strategic purchasing: A history and review of the literature. *International Journal of Purchasing and Materials Management, 30*(2), 1–9.

Ellram, L. M., Tate, W., & Billington, C. (2004). Understanding and managing the services supply chain. *The Journal of Supply Chain Management, 40*(4), 17–32.

Ellram, L. M., Tate, W. L., & Billington, C. (2007). Services supply management: The next frontier for improved organizational performance. *California Management Review, 49*(4), 44–66.

Fitzsimmons, J. A., & Fitzsimmons, M. J. (2006). *Service management: Operations, strategy, and information technology* (5th ed.). McGraw Hill.

Giannakis, M., Dubey, R., Vlachos, I., & Ju, Y. (2020). Supplier sustainability performance evaluation using the analytic network process. *Journal of Cleaner Production, 247*, 119439.

Jordan, C., & Bak, O. (2016). The growing scale and scope of the supply chain: A reflection on supply chain graduate skills. *Supply Chain Management, 21*(5), 610–626.

Kraljic, P. (1983). Purchasing must become supply management. *Harvard Business Review, (September-October, 1983), pp.* 110–117.

Küffner, C., Münch, C., Hähner, S., & Hartmann, E. (2022). Getting back into the swing of things: The adaptive path of purchasing and supply management in enhancing supply chain resilience. *Journal of Purchasing and Supply Management, 28*(5), 100802.

Lorentz, H., Töyli, J., Solakivi, T., & Ojala, L. (2013). Priorities and determinants for supply chain management skills development in manufacturing firms. *Supply Chain Management: An International Journal, 18*(4), 358–375.

Maestrini, V., Luzzini, D., Caniato, F., Maccarrone, P., & Ronchi, S. (2018). The impact of supplier performance measurement systems on supplier performance: A dyadic lifecycle perspective. *International Journal of Operations & Production Management, 38*(11), 2040–2061.

Mangan, J., & Christopher, M. (2005). Management development and the supply chain manager of the future. *The International Journal of Logistics Management, 16*(2), 178–191.

Monczka, R., Trent, R., & Handfield, R. (2005). *Purchasing and supply chain management* (3rd ed.). Thomson South-Western.

Pereira, C. R. (2014). The Role of Procurement in Creating Supply Chain Resilience (PhD thesis). Federal University of Sao Carlos, Sao Carlos, Brazil. Available at: https://repositorio.ufscar.br/handle/ufscar/3451(Last accessed: 31.05.2024).

Pereira, C. R., Christopher, M., & Silva, A. L. (2014). Achieving supply chain resilience: The role of procurement. *Supply Chain Management: An International Journal, 19*(5/6), 626–642.

Pereira, C. R., da Silva, A. L., Tate, W. L., & Christopher, M. (2020). Purchasing and supply management (PSM) contribution to supply-side resilience. *International Journal of Production Economics, 228*, 107740.

Prajogo, D., & Sohal, A. (2013). Supply chain professionals: A study of competencies, use of technologies, and future challenges. *International Journal of Operations & Production Management, 33*(11/12), 1532–1554.

Schmelzle, U., Pellathy, D. A., Tate, W. L., & Min, J. (2023). The conductor matters: The impact of purchasing orchestration on organizational performance. *Journal of Global Operations and Strategic Sourcing*, Ahead-of-print.

Schmelzle, U., & Tate, W. (2022). Purchasing orchestration practices – Introducing a purchasing-innovation framework. *Journal of Purchasing and Supply Management, 28*(2), 100756.

Schoenherr, T., Modi, S. B., Benton, W. C., Carter, C. R., Choi, T. Y., Larson, P. D., & Wagner, S. M. (2012). Research opportunities in purchasing and supply management. *International Journal of Production Research, 50*(16), 4556–4579.

Schulze, H., Bals, L., & Johnsen, T. E. (2019). Individual competences for sustainable purchasing and supply management (SPSM). *International Journal of Physical Distribution & Logistics Management, 49*(3), 287–304.

Sobhani, M., Malarvizhi, C. A., Al-Mamun, A., & Jeyashree, S. (2014). Strategic procurement and financial performance of Iranian manufacturing companies. *Asian Social Science, 10*(1), 250–256.

Wisner, J. D., & Stanley, L. L. (2008). *Process management: Creating value along the supply chain*. International Student Edition.

Zsidisin, G. A., Panelli, A., & Upton, R. (2000). Purchasing organization involvement in risk assessments, contingency plans, and risk management: An exploratory study. *Supply Chain Management, 5*(4), 187–197.

CHAPTER 4

Resilience in Service Supply Chains

Abstract In Chapter 4, the concept of resilience is discussed, shedding light on its key meaning within the areas of operations and supply chain management (O&SCM). In doing so, this paper discusses the three perspectives of resilience (engineering, ecological, and social-ecological), the bundle of elements of resilience, and how risk and vulnerability are interrelated concepts of resilience. The chapter ends by providing a range of examples of resilience in the service industry and supply chain.

Keywords Concept of resilience · Engineering resilience · Ecological resilience · Social-ecological resilience · Elements of resilience · Resilience in service

Building a resilient supply chain is currently one of the most frequently discussed topics among researchers and practitioners. However, most of the strategies suggested thus far have been explored through a tangible product lens, and little has been explored through a service perspective. Therefore, in this chapter, we will first cover the concept of resilience and its current understanding within the supply chain context before examining how this concept can be used in the service sector.

C. Pereira and Ö. Yurt, *Achieving Resilience in Service Supply Chains*, Palgrave Studies in Logistics and Supply Chain Management,
https://doi.org/10.1007/978-3-031-68244-5_4

4.1 Resilience in Operations and Supply Chains

Not long ago, resilience was not a word used or heard on a daily basis, especially in the business area. It has its roots in different disciplines, such as psychology, ecology, and material science, which reflects its multi-faceted nature. A common example of resilience is when referring to a "spring" as a flexible and adaptable material (material science perspective) or commenting on the individual capacity to recover from difficult life-experience situations (psychological perspective). In each of these areas, the meaning of resilience is quite similar in the sense that it brings up the ideas of disruption, deformation, recovery, and transformation. Figure 4.1 illustrates some core definitions of resilience across different disciplines, fields, or domains.

According to all of these definitions, the presence of a phenomenon that triggers the development of resilience—disruption—is noticeable. Thus, given the multitude of disruptive events occurring in recent decades (e.g., public health crises, climate-related incidents, geopolitical and religious conflicts, and technological advancements), the concept of resilience has been intensively discussed by practitioners and scholars in the O&SCM area. The tipping points for the boom of interest around "resilience" in the business context were remarkable events such as the UK fuel protest in September 2000 (Davey & Macaskill, 2021; Davis, 2021), foot and mouth disease in February 2001 in the UK (BBC News, 2011), and the US terrorist attack in September 2001 (Jackson, 2021). This, therefore, drove the exploitation of this concept to help organisations and their entire supply chains address the increasing number of risks and potential disruptions worldwide (as presented in Chapter 2).

Seminal studies such as Christopher and Peck (2004), Sheffi and Rice (2005), and Ponomarov and Holcomb (2009) inspired ideas and research to progress towards a common understanding of resilience and envisage future opportunities for advanced practice to achieve business continuity and long-term sustainability. Considering that resilience is subjected to changes in operation mode, Sheffi and Rice (2005) identify eight steps that organisations usually pass through after a disruptive event in their operations (Fig. 4.2). They state that organisations should be able to return to their normal performance quicker if they have prepared themselves to deal with a variety of disruptions (e.g., through developing good contingency plans) and can make timely decisions and actions to overcome these impacts. Hence, the recovery phase can last shorter or longer

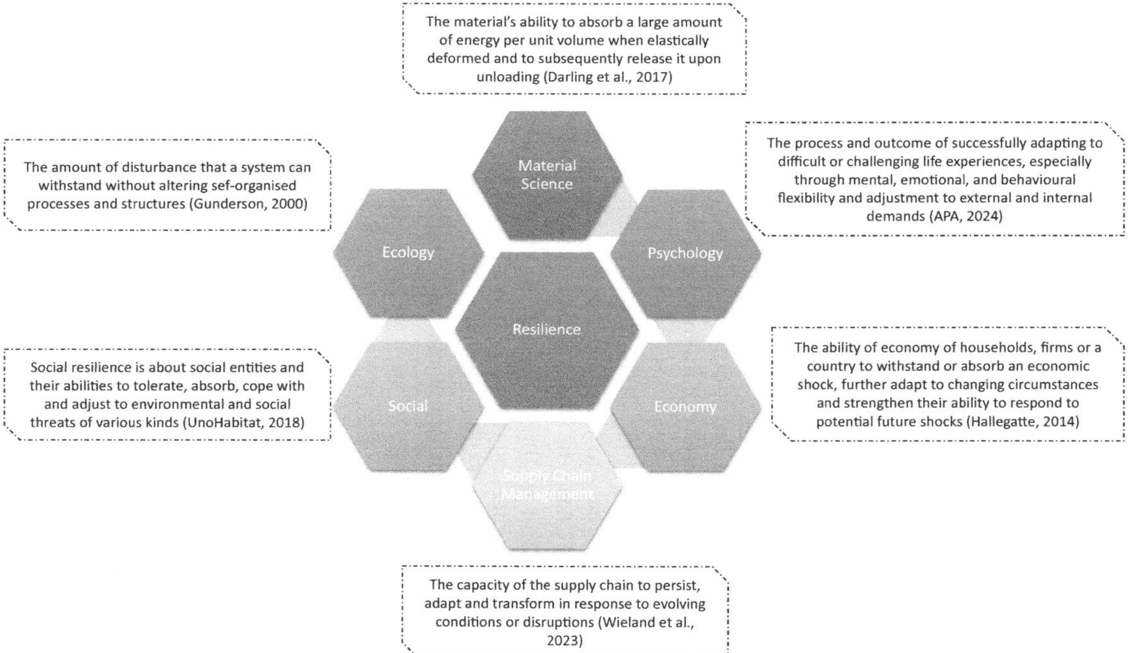

Fig. 4.1 Definitions of resilience across different disciplines, fields, or domains. *Source: Authors generated based on the references listed in the figure*

depending on the company's actions during and after the impact. In this regard, authors (e.g., Ali et al., 2017; Jüttner & Maklan, 2011; Ponomarov & Holcomb, 2009; Spiegler et al., 2012; Wright, 2013) state three phases to achieve resilience: preparedness, response, and recovery.

Finally, how organisations address disruptions by effectively using their resources over time will define how resilient they are. For those who are able to recover, the disruption may have different impacts—some will continue their operations lower than expected (continuous line following the initial stage in Fig. 4.2), some will bounce back to their original state of operations (middle dash-dotted line at the end of Fig. 4.2), and some will excel in the original state by taking the disruption as an opportunity to adapt and transform their business (top dash-dotted line at the end of Fig. 4.2).

By acknowledging the multiple actions and strategies to be taken during the different phases of disruptions, resilience is seen as a dynamic concept because, through a variety of innovative actions, it can change the system and adapt it to distinct situations and scenarios. Nevertheless, there are authors (e.g., Annarelli et al., 2020; Pettit et al., 2010) who distinguish resilience into static and dynamic states. Static resilience involves only the preparedness phase, in which preventive measures are taken to minimise threats in terms of the probability of occurrence and potential impacts. Dynamic resilience, on the other hand, covers the remaining two phases and focuses on the effective management of unforeseen events to shorten unfavourable aftermaths and maximise the organisation's speed of recovery (Fig. 4.2).

4.1.1 The Different Perspectives of Resilience

The body of resilience literature expands, prompting the continual evolution of this concept. Recent studies have endeavoured to explore resilience through the lenses of different disciplines (as shown in Fig. 4.1). Table 4.1, therefore, lists the evolution of resilience definitions in the literature on O&SCM, where different levels of analysis and perspectives are considered, as discussed below.

The initial perspective adopted by the authors in defining resilience is rooted in engineering principles. This viewpoint supposes a single stable state or equilibrium to which the system is expected to "bounce back". Holling (1996) defines *engineering resilience* as a system that bounces back to its original state once the disruption has passed or been removed.

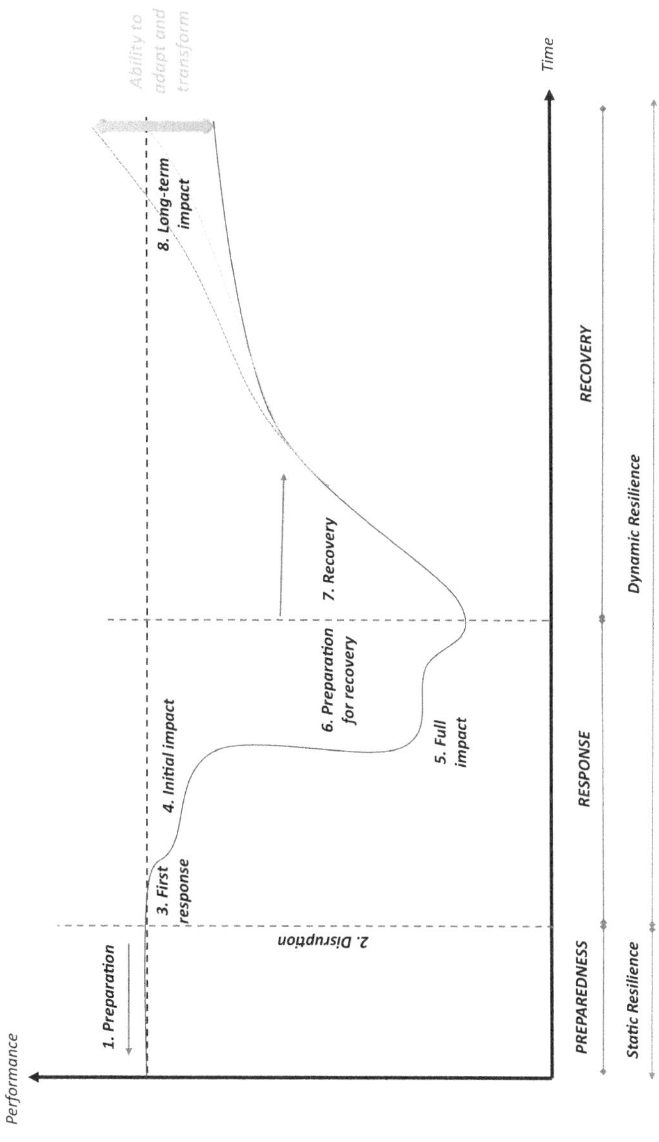

Fig. 4.2 Stages of disruptions in a resilient supply chain. *Source: Authors generated based on* Ponomarov and Holcomb (2009), Jüttner and Maklan (2011), Spiegler et al. (2012), *and* Wright (2013)

Table 4.1 Key definitions of resilience in operations and supply chains

Authors	*Resilience definition*	*Level of analysis*	*Perspectives of Resilience*
Christopher and Peck (2004, p.2)	It is the ability of a system to return to its original state or move to a new, more desirable state after being disturbed	System	Ecological
Sheffi and Rice (2005, p.41)	It is the firm's ability to absorb disruptions or enable the supply chain network to return to state conditions faster and thus has a positive impact on firm performance	Firm/ Supply Chain	Engineering
Fiksel (2006, p.16)	The capacity for an enterprise to survive, adapt, and grow in the face of turbulent change	Firm	Ecological
Ponomarov and Holcomb (2009, p.131)	The adaptive capability of the supply chain to prepare for unexpected events, respond to disruptions, and recover from them by maintaining continuity of operations at the desired level of connectedness and control over structure and function	Supply Chain	Engineering
Pettit et al., (2010, p.1)	The capacity for an enterprise to survive, adapt and grow in the face of turbulent change	Supply Chain	Ecological
Carvalho et al. (2012)	Resilience is referred to as the ability of supply chains to cope with unexpected disturbances	Supply Chain	Engineering
Urciuoli et al. (2014)	The capability of companies to anticipate, identify, react and learn from incidents	Firm	Ecological
Fiksel et al. (2014)	[...] resilience, the adaptive capacity of a system, includes the ability to transform. It goes beyond buffers and spare capacity; it enables the system not just to react but actually to reconfigure itself in response to a shock	System	Ecological
Tukamuhabwa et al. (2015)	The adaptive capability of a supply chain to prepare for and/or respond to disruptions, to make a timely and cost-effective recovery, and therefore progress to a post disruption state of operations	Supply Chain	Engineering

(continued)

Table 4.1 (continued)

Authors	*Resilience definition*	*Level of analysis*	*Perspectives of Resilience*
Scholten and Schilder (2015)	Resilience enables a supply chain to be prepared for events and reduce the impact of a disruption and strengthens the ability to recover quickly from them by maintaining continuity of operations at the desired level of connectedness and control over structure and function	Supply Chain	Engineering
Kamalahamadi and Parast (2016)	The adaptive capability of a supply chain to reduce the probability of facing sudden disturbances resist the spread of disturbances by maintaining control over structures and functions and recover and respond by immediate and effective reactive plans to transcend the disturbance and restore the supply chains to a robust state of operations	Supply Chain	Engineering
Dabhilkar et al. (2016)	Return to, or maintain continuity of, operations at the desired level of connectedness and control over structure and function	Firm	Engineering
Novak et al., (2021, p.332)	A supply chain is resilient to the extent that the system can maintain core functionality by continually adapting, evolving, and transforming in response to the dynamic multiscale feedbacks that occur between the multitude of interconnected organisations, institutions, and social and ecological systems that are all parts of the larger supply chain	System	Social-Ecological
Wieland and Durach (2021, p.316)	Supply chain resilience is the capacity of a supply chain to persist, adapt, or transform in the face of change	Supply Chain	Social-Ecological
Essuman et al., (2023, p.302)	Resilience can manifest in a system's ability to absorb, recover from, adapt to, or transform in response to disruptions	System	Social-Ecological

In this context, resilience is characterised as the firm's capacity to detect disruptions, mitigate their consequences by absorbing them, and endure the impact of a shock, thereby preserving both structure and function (Vega et al., 2023). This perspective also focuses on gauging the firm's ability to recover swiftly from a disruption, with greater system resilience correlating with faster recovery (Novak et al., 2021). Consequently, metrics such as "time-to-recover" and "time-to-survive" have been introduced to assess supply chain resilience (Simchi-Levi et al., 2015; Wieland, 2020). Definitions based on engineering principles align with the concepts of elasticity and the system's capability to absorb shocks while sustaining critical structures (Simmie & Martin, 2010).

Table 4.1 presents several definitions that focus on managing structure, process, and function (e.g., Kamalahamadi & Parast, 2016; Ponomarov & Holcomb, 2009; Scholten & Schilder, 2015), which are timely and cost-effective (Sheffi & Rice, 2005; Tukamuhabwa et al., 2015). However, recent studies by authors such as Wieland and Durach (2021), Wieland et al. (2023), and others have contended that the engineering assumptions of maintaining a steady-state equilibrium may oversimplify the intricate reality of nonlinear, uncertain, and unexpected behaviours in the complex environment of today's global supply chains (Davis-Sramek & Richey, 2021).

In the literature, a second perspective known as *ecological resilience* has emerged, exploring the dynamics of systems as they shift and adapt to alternative steady states. This perspective specifically investigates the capacity of ecological systems or organisms to persist and adapt to disruptions. Consider, for instance, the annual cycle of trees shedding and regrowing leaves in response to changing seasons. Ecological resilience recognises that systems may possess multiple equilibria, and returning to a preshock operating baseline might not be desirable, practical, or feasible. In this context, the concept of the "new normal" encapsulates the essence of ecological resilience.

The assessment of ecological resilience involves considering the magnitude of disturbance a system can absorb (its buffering capacity) before fundamental processes or structures undergo changes, leading the system to transition to alternative equilibrium (Novak et al., 2021). However, both aforementioned perspectives view resilience as a closed system with various states of equilibrium (Umar & Wilson, 2023). It can be argued that this perspective may not hold in the case of complex systems such as food chains, where interconnected social, political, economic, and environmental factors continually shape the actions and adaptability of various components (Wieland & Durach, 2021).

The prevailing social-ecological perspective, widely embraced by contemporary authors, arises from the recognition that systems such as forests, cities, and communities are inherently open and complex.

In contrast to the conventional closed-system approaches predominant in engineering (Wieland et al., 2023), the social-ecological viewpoint perceives resilience as a characteristic of a system with the capacity for continual adaptation and transformation in response to multiscale feedback and shocks (Novak et al., 2021). In essence, it embodies the concept of "changing in order not to be changed" (Walker, 2020, p.11), emphasising nonlinear dynamics, uncertainty, thresholds, and surprises. This perspective delves into how periods of rapid change intersect with gradual change and examines the intricate interplay of such dynamic processes (Wieland & Durach, 2021).

Within this perspective, Wieland et al. (2023) assert that resilience extends beyond mere **persistence**—a notion aligned with the engineering-based view that involves sustained efforts to achieve goals despite difficulties, failures, or opposition. Instead, it encompasses **adaptation**, the adjustment of existing systems in response to actual or anticipated changes or disruptions, and **transformation**, the radical alteration of a system's structures and processes in response to evolving conditions or disruptions (Wieland et al., 2023, p.3). This perspective, named the *social-ecological perspective*, holds particular relevance in current business scenarios, acknowledging that disturbances not only challenge but also drive opportunities for innovation and development.

Figure 4.3 illustrates these three perspectives of resilience through the simple representation of different systems, which could be focused on a physical good or a service. Drawing on the adaptive cycle as a foundational concept for understanding ongoing adaptation and transformation, Wieland (2020), Vega et al. (2023), and other authors explore how the reconfiguration of the supply chain's structure, processes, norms, and routines results in the utilisation of new resources or different uses of previously owned resources. This perspective thus serves as a distinguished lens through which to navigate the dynamic landscape of business resilience in the face of evolving disruptions and new ways of doing business (in which service is a prominent one).

The social-ecological perspective is easily observed through businesses' reactions after COVID-19. This disruptive event pushed entire supply chains beyond their comfort zones, compelling a re-evaluation of strategies for survival. Many examples have emerged in response. In Brazil, Kidy, a renowned footwear industry for children, promptly adapted by reallocating a portion of its production to manufacture face masks (Kidy Calçados, 2020). Similarly, DeMillus, the largest manufacturer of female

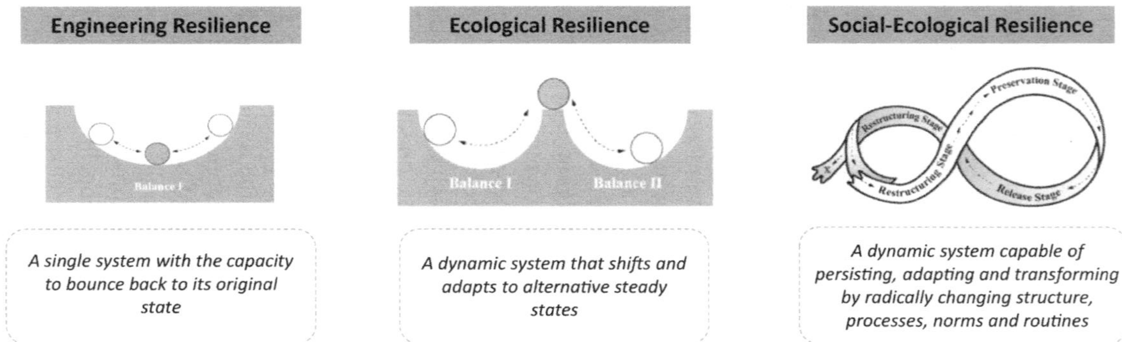

Fig. 4.3 Three perspectives of resilience *Source: Based on concepts and ideas from* Wu et al. (2022) *and* Vega et al. (2023)

underwear, utilised its textile expertise and resources to redirect 50% of its production towards crafting face masks and disposable triple nonwoven coats, primarily intended for hospital supply (ABIT, 2020).

Mercedes-Benz Brazil demonstrated agility and collaboration by entering a partnership with a respirator manufacturer to accelerate production (Mercedes-Benz Cars & Vans Brasil, 2020). Pioneira, specialising in equipment for cleaning, gardening, and reforestation, extended its efforts beyond its usual scope to include the daily disinfection of streets, hospitals, and emergency rooms in Suzano, a city in the metropolitan region of São Paulo (Globo News, 2020). By deploying two water tankers daily, they sprayed a hygiene-promoting liquid strategically aimed at reducing the risk of contamination in areas with significant foot traffic. The Espírito Santo cosmetics industry, Ervas Naturais in Vila Velha, also responded dynamically to the crisis by redirecting its entire manufacturing structure to produce hand sanitisers throughout April and mid-March 2020 (Nicácio et al., 2020).

Turkish companies from various sectors have adapted their operations and strategies to respond to the challenges posed by the COVID-19 pandemic, showcasing the social-ecological perspective in action. For instance, Turkish Airlines, in response to a substantial decline in passenger travel, redirected its attention to cargo operations. The airline deployed its fleet to transport medical supplies, personal protective equipment, and other vital commodities worldwide. This strategic shift not only facilitated the functioning of worldwide supply chains but also ensured the continued operation of the airline amidst a decline in passenger travel (THY, 2020). Additionally, Arçelik, a prominent maker of household appliances, promptly responded to the COVID-19 issue by manufacturing mechanical ventilators. Arçelik collaborated with local enterprises and utilised its engineering expertise to commence the production of ventilators, with the aim of providing assistance to hospitals and the healthcare system in Turkey (Nasdaq, 2020).

Whether motivated by survival or helping the global community, they not only successfully adapted to a temporary crisis but also acquired valuable lessons to support continuous innovation in their business in the long term. According to Davis-Sramek and Richey (2021), this perspective seems to share some common ground with Craighead et al. (2020), who define "transilience" as the capacity to simultaneously restore certain processes and radically transform others. A notable distinction, however, is that the authors situate transilience within the context of pandemics, emphasising its distinctiveness from typical supply chain disruptions.

All these perspectives of resilience, whichever they are adopted by manufacturing or service organisations, can exist at multiple levels: organisational, buyer–supplier dyad, supply base, supply network, or collections of supply networks. Each of these is not mutually exclusive but rather coexists at any moment in time (Azadegan & Dooley, 2021). As they are all interconnected, many manufacturing firms had to implement manufacturing-level strategies to address the production change caused by the pandemic to keep their supply chains up and running (Dwaikat et al., 2022). This, therefore, calls for different principles or elements of resilience (e.g., collaboration, information sharing, and agility) to be developed and/or applied by practitioners (especially procurement and supply chain management ones) to create resilience capability throughout the whole supply chain.

4.1.2 Elements of Resilience

Another topic within the concept of resilience that has long been extensively discussed in the literature thus far is the elements of resilience (e.g., Christopher & Peck, 2004; Sheffi & Rice, 2005; Wieland et al., 2023; Ivanov, 2020; Akbar& Aslam, 2023), which covers the idea of "what drives resilience". Authors, therefore, use different terminologies, such as principles (Christopher & Peck, 2004), enablers (Pereira et al., 2014), factors (Ambulkar et al., 2015), capabilities (Pettit et al., 2010), and elements (Ali et al., 2017; Costa et al., 2019, 2022; Karl et al., 2018). The term "elements of resilience" (EoR) will be used in this book following the work of Ali et al. (2017), who developed a comprehensive concept mapping framework to classify different terminologies of resilience across papers in the O&SCM area. Table 4.2 summarises the most discussed EoR from several studies identified in the literature.

4.1.3 Risk and Vulnerability as Interlinked Concepts to Resilience

As previously mentioned, the tipping points for the development of resilience capability lie in unexpected and disruptive events, which normally evolve through different types of risks (ranging from low to high probability) and the preparedness of organisations for vulnerabilities. Therefore, the consequences or impacts of disruptions result from the

Table 4.2 Elements of resilience

Element of Resilience	*Description*
Agility	This is the organisation's ability to react quickly to changing circumstances, challenges, and disruptions. It is triggered by developing other elements of resilience, such as flexibility or redundancy
Alignment	Aligning involves ensuring that key variables of an organisation (such as demand forecasting or purchasing orders, incentives, and risks) are coordinated and working towards common goals (organisations and supply chain partners). This is important to achieving supply chain collaboration and consequently effectively responding to disruptions at a system level
Collaboration	Collaborative working among sourcing parties or among employees helps to exchange information and improve the willingness to help each other, creating responsiveness
Trust	Reliability among organisations is a key enabler of collaboration, visibility, information sharing, and risk mitigation, which are indispensable for adapting to and recovering from disruptions
Coordination & Control	Effective coordination ensures that all parts work together seamlessly, while control involves monitoring and guiding actions to stay aligned with common and agreed objectives. Therefore, supply chain organisations need to be capable of coordinating and controlling their processes and flows to better manage resources, especially during disruptions
Company's Knowledge	Companies that have extensive knowledge about their products' end-to-end flows are able to make more conscientious decisions and back up their knowledge with previous experiences
Flexibility	Flexible products, processes, and transportation, for instance, provide a wider range of options for managers to replace the interrupted flows and consequently take more responsive action
Financial Strength	Capacity to absorb fluctuations in cash flow and support the creation of resilience, which is known as a costly capability by creating redundancy and flexibility, for instance
Information Sharing	It involves the timely and transparent exchange of relevant information (that could be in any form of data, insights, and knowledge) between and among supply chain partners. This ensures that organisations have access to up-to-date information, which helps in assertive decision-making. Information sharing is a key element to achieving resilience because it enhances visibility, coordination, and alignment
Integration	Integration seeks to develop good relationships among business functions and the demand and supply sides, which increases organisational performance by increasing information sharing
Redundancy	Having extra capacity options, such as inventory or suppliers, can make companies more resilient in terms of their ability to change the normal direction of flows quickly

(continued)

Table 4.2 (continued)

Element of Resilience	*Description*
Risk Management	Risk identification, assessment, and monitoring are key activities that companies should develop to understand the potential risks around the business and their own vulnerabilities and develop mitigation actions. Risks could also be shared between supply chain partners
Supply Chain Design	Redesigning the supply chain is a key element that can potentially make companies more responsive by focusing on the location strategies of suppliers, customers, or their own settings
Velocity and Acceleration	According to Physics, velocity is defined as distance over time, and acceleration is velocity over time. These two factors are very important for creating quick responses in disruptive scenarios. These elements are also closely linked to flexibility and agility
Visibility	Being able to visualise both the demand and supply sides is key to allowing managers to make safe decisions, assess possible risks, and find ways to cope with them. In addition, achieving this enabler makes it easier to manage resources and change strategies in case of disruptions

interplay of these two variables (risk and vulnerability), which are widely acknowledged concepts in the literature on O&SCM, as exemplified by Sheffi and Rice (2005) and Pettit et al., (2010, 2019).

Numerous internal, external, and environmental risks can make companies and their supply chains vulnerable, including complex networks, extended lead times, and plant locations. In this sense, Christopher and Peck (2004, p.6) define vulnerability as "an exposure to serious disturbance, arising from risks within the supply chain as well as risks external to the supply chain". The same authors, supported by many other subsequent studies (e.g., Ali et al., 2017; Jüttner & Maklan, 2011; Maslaric et al., 2013;), explain that there are many interpretations of risk in the literature, but the most commonly used interpretation in the O&SCM context is hazard-focused interpretation, in which risk is understood as the probability (of a given event occurring) versus the severity (negative business impact) of disruptions.

High levels of vulnerability are present when the disruption probability (likelihood) and impact (consequences) are both high—causing critical and severe disruptions. Conversely, low levels of vulnerability are created from a combination of low disruption probability and mild consequences, which are typically associated with daily activities—causing controlled or serious disruptions. Disruptive results are generated by an average and dynamic level of disruption probability and impact. In risk management terms, these middle-ground disruptions require balanced attention—they are significant enough to warrant preparation and mitigation efforts but not so extreme as to necessitate the highest levels of precaution or intervention.

Therefore, risk and vulnerability are concepts often addressed together to assess the consequences and impacts of disruptions, and they compose a powerful tool for organisations, namely, risk assessment (Fig. 4.4). While this matrix suggests that critical events are those with both high probability and high impact levels, it is important to note that even low probability events can lead to serious impacts. Companies that place low priority on an event are more likely not to be prepared for it, and as a result, they may face significant impacts. In Sect. 4.2, there are a few examples that fall into this category, such as COVID-19 and the Suez Canal incident.

In some of the literature, there is a degree of confusion in statements concerning vulnerability and risk. According to Sheffi and Rice (2005, p.41), "reducing vulnerability means reducing the likelihood of a disruption and increasing resilience". However, this assertion is not universally applicable, considering that likelihood is an attribute of risks and may sometimes be beyond avoidance or prediction. Consequently, it cannot be guaranteed that diminishing risk renders a supply chain less vulnerable or more resilient. Making a supply chain unique or adaptable could indeed enhance its resilience. Ponomarov and Holcomb (2009, p.129) elucidate this notion by stating that "the vulnerability of infrastructure could be decreased during the recovery stage (e.g., a bridge destroyed by an earthquake could be replaced by a new one with a better and more robust design)". Consequently, there is an emphasis on building on different strategies, such as product or service specifications or network redesign.

In the face of minor disruptions, for instance, bolstering robustness serves as a viable option to protect against small impacts and ensure business continuity. However, in regard to major disruptions, companies should cultivate resilient practices to swiftly transform their original operations to mitigate the risk of substantial economic losses. In this sense, Zsidisin et al. (2000) posit that every business environment inherently carries a degree of risk, and while internal measures may mitigate some of these risks, organisations should create additional strategies to handle unforeseeable incidents. Therefore, although the conventional risk assessment approach holds significance, it falls short when confronted

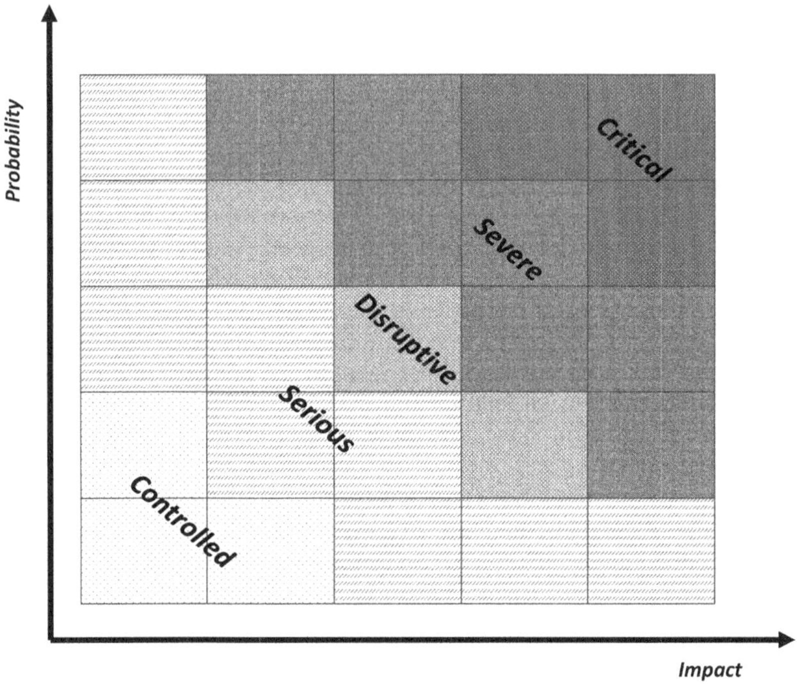

Fig. 4.4 The risk assessment matrix *Source: Authors generated based on Kassem et al.* (2019) and Acebes et al. (2024)

with unpredictable events. Consequently, there is a belief that supply chain resilience can complement existing risk management programmes. In support of this, Pettit et al., (2010, p.4) assert that "resilience is an evolving concept and differs from traditional risk management".

A commonly posed question concerning resilience is "Are the necessary investments worth it?" Increasing resilience often requires financial investments, and quantifying the return on investment is not a straightforward activity for organisations. However, although fortifying resilience in the supply chain may not be a cost-effective strategy, it is pivotal to develop adaptive and transformation actions to address an array of events (regardless of their probability or impact). Additionally, the prevailing trend of organisations towards minimal costs has shifted. With a greater awareness of current challenges, they are investing more in their businesses to enhance safety and competitiveness. The upcoming chapter delves deeper into this trade-off.

4.2 Resilience in Service Supply Chains

Services should flow across supply chains, even under adverse conditions, to increase resilience. Let us consider a few examples of disruptive events.

One of the typical but powerful examples to contextualise this is the NHS supply chain in the UK during the COVID-19 pandemic. The urgent need for protective equipment (PPE), ventilators, and other medical supplies, along with how these supplies were supplied, were the main issues that had to be solved by supply chain professionals. Relevant supply chain processes, such as order management, inventory management, and demand forecasting, also had to be managed smoothly, at least from a physical goods perspective. This was not an easy task, clearly. However, the more critical part was ensuring that all required medical staff were ready to offer the service—physically, mentally, and emotionally. As previously discussed, in a service encounter, the service buyer (patient in this case) and the provider (medical staff) must exist at the same time. Hence, to achieve service supply chain resilience, we must properly and urgently manage all the functions of the service supply chain, including capacity and resource management, demand management, customer relationship management, and supplier relationship management. The overarching role of information management must remain here as well.

Similarly, from a humanitarian supply chain perspective, recent earthquakes in Turkey and Syria (in February 2023) made it impossible to transport healthcare from or to facilities. Energy and communication were also disrupted, leading to major challenges in ordering or delivering medical supplies and services (Pearson, 2023). Despite these difficulties, service supply chain strategies have become paramount for building resilience. Enhanced coordination among relief agencies, for instance, was an essential action for optimising the use of available resources.

On the other hand, the literature is rich in examples of disruptions caused by different sources but typically focuses on the product side. Nevertheless, as highlighted in Chapter 2, all manufacturing organisations have a great deal of service embedded in their operations. Dell is one example of this, and it has a well-documented case regarding resilience due to its strategies for dealing with critical events. Following Sheffi's (2005, p.225) comprehensive description of this case, a powerful earthquake with a magnitude of 7.6 struck Taiwan in September 1999, affecting the nation's high-tech manufacturing sector. Although the earthquake caused the deaths of thousands of people, it did not significantly damage the 28 semiconductor manufacturing plants in the park. However, the manufacturers experienced a power outage lasting nearly 24 hours, which led to the loss of tens of thousands of wafers (one of the key components for producing chips used in computers). As a result, it took several weeks for manufacturers to restore their operations and return to pre-earthquake chip production yields.

Taiwan was responsible for producing 10–15% of the world's dynamic random access memory (DRAM) chips, 80% of the graphics chips, and 60% of computer mainboards, not to mention the liquid crystal display (LCD) suppliers and assemblers. This means that the earthquake's disruption quickly impacted the chip makers' customers, which included major computer manufacturers, such as Hewlett-Packard (HP), Compaq, IBM, Dell, Siemens, Fujitsu, and Apple. This ripple effect led to disruptions in computer production and delivery, affecting end customers in various ways depending on each computer maker's manufacturing processes and customer relations.

Companies that suffered the most from a shortage of chips were those using lean production systems (minimal inventory due to a just-in-time supply of components such as memory chips, circuit boards, and laptop screens). In this case, two leading companies with lean built-up-to-order systems experienced different outcomes. Apple Computer, Inc., operates a build-to-order supply and manufacturing system; however, at that time, it was launching a new series of computers (iBook and G4 Power Macintosh) and published the configurations and prices in advance for loyal and high-tech customers to preorder the machines. Unfortunately, this led to a misstep for Apple as they ended up committing themselves to produce and deliver over 160,000 iBooks in advance. When the earthquake hit, Apple had delivered only a small portion of the preordered iBooks. Adding to Apple's challenges, another supplier was unable to deliver the required volumes of the fastest G4 processors. As a result, Apple chose to downgrade customers rather than face significant shipping delays for computers with the correct configuration. This led to widespread customer dissatisfaction, prompting many to cancel their orders. As a result, Apple experienced significant financial impact due to lost orders and reduced sales margins.

On the other hand, Dell (a pioneer in the build-to-order business model) manages its supply chain by assembling computers at the very stage when customers place their orders in a highly customised way. Therefore, by employing a well-conducted "make-to-order" system and postponing its product assembly, which allows for adjustments in the configuration and price, Dell has maintained its operations running and, hence, taking over Apple's market share (Christopher & Holweg, 2011). From a service perspective, Dell's resilience strategies lie in effectively utilising a "make-to-order" system and postponing product assembly. These strategies are particularly relevant in the service industry because Dell primarily operates in the domain of providing customisable and personalised computer products, which could be considered part of an information and communication technology service.

Let us reflect on this case but now take the service side of it.

1. **Make-to-Order Approach**
    - *Customer-Centric Approach:* The "make-to-order" system is customer-centric, which, for instance, allows Dell to tailor products according to individual customer specifications. This aligns with a service-oriented mindset, where customisation and meeting specific customer needs are paramount to keeping operations running and preventing unexpected disruptions.
    - *Reduced Inventory and Waste:* This approach minimises the need for extensive prebuilt inventory, thereby reducing excess stock and the cash invested in it. For example, Dell was able to efficiently respond to customer demands in real time by adjusting component availability on the website, avoiding stockouts. This enhanced the agility of its service provision.
2. **Postponement of Product Assembly:**
    - *Flexibility and Adaptability:* By postponing product assembly until specific customer orders are received, Dell gained flexibility and adaptability in responding to market changes. This approach resonates with the dynamic nature of services, where the ability to adapt quickly to evolving customer requirements is essential.

- *Configuration Adjustments:* This enabled Dell to make last-minute configuration adjustments based on their supply availability, aligning the final product with customer preferences. This mirrors the service industry's need to stay current and responsive to changing customer expectations.

3. **Competitiveness and Performance**

- *Market Responsiveness:* Dell's resilience is demonstrated through its ability to stay competitive by swiftly adjusting product configurations and prices.
- *Performance Sustainability:* Continually adapting product configurations ensures that Dell can sustain its performance by offering products that meet evolving market demands. This is a significant aspect of resilience in the service sector, where customer satisfaction is critical to long-term success.

Moving forward, diverse disruptions can impact businesses in various ways. Similarly, we can consider another example from Sheffi (2005) and Sheffi and Rice (2005). The authors provide an intriguing viewpoint on McDonald's outlets. Despite incidents of attacks and protests in countries such as France, Canada, and Turkey, suggesting that this fast-food chain may face a greater risk of attacks due to its association with "Americanism", McDonald's stores are not particularly vulnerable to being shut down by local terrorist attacks. This is because of the redundancy of having numerous nearby stores. However, they are highly vulnerable to outbreaks of mad cow disease or other issues that could undermine consumer confidence.

In parallel with McDonald's strategic redundancy against local terrorist attacks and the United States Postal Office (USPS) soon after the 9/11 terrorist attack, it is possible to take advantage of the redundancy strategy by having multiple postal offices across the country.

> *"Between September 18 and October 9, 2001, a series of letters were deposited at a mailbox in New Jersey. Poison-pen letters in a very literal sense, the envelopes contained a fine powder of deadly anthrax spores [...] As these letters made their way to their fateful destinations, they left behind a deadly residue. Sent to addresses in New York, Washington, D.C., and Florida, the letters entered the United States Postal Service's (USPS) massive network. The fine anthrax dust leaked from the envelopes to contaminate the Brentwood Processing and Distribution Center in Washington D.C., the Trenton*

Processing and Distribution Center in New Jersey, and a host of minor mail handling facilities in New Jersey, New York, Washington, and Florida." (Sheffi, 2005, *p.171).*

Not underestimating the personal and social impact that this terrorist attack caused to U.S. families, during that period, the USPS had to ensure that mail delivery continued despite Brentwood's closure. The USPS rerouted mail to two other distribution centres, which resulted in parcel delivery that normally resumed the day after Brentwood closed. The USPS managed the closure of the Brentwood facility, as well as the Trenton facility and other smaller facilities, due to overcapacity in its system. This redundancy was not planned for disasters but resulted from decreased mail volume due to the increasing use of the internet. Because USPS workers are protected by civil service employment laws, the USPS cannot quickly adjust its operations, leading to this overcapacity. Although not all service companies can afford to maintain idle capacity, this strategy can help them overcome critical disruptions such as this one.

Unlike a localised incident, such as the previous examples of terrorist attacks, the global nature of the COVID-19 pandemic transformed the way many service businesses used to operate. For instance, hotels were highly impacted because they had to shut down the service for a few months, and even after the initial waves of the pandemic, when the restrictions were eased, hotels still had low occupancy, in addition to stringent health and safety protocols across all their facilities, ensuring sanitation. Additionally, they focused on transparent communication about their preventive measures, showcasing a commitment to guest well-being. The hotel chain also invested in technologies, such as contactless check-in and enhanced cleaning procedures, to adapt to the changing expectations of travellers in the post-COVID era (Pillai et al., 2021). Most accommodation platforms, such as Booking.com and Airbnb, have implemented a "Health & Safety" filter to reassure guests that the room has been thoroughly cleaned and sanitised according to COVID-19 measures (Airbnb, n.d.; Booking.com, n.d; Bull, 2020).

Therefore, to implement resilient strategies in hotels, broader concerns related to the impacts of the pandemic should be addressed to adapt to the new normal of travel in the post-COVID landscape. For example, Accor and Marriott hotels in Thailand have implemented strategic measures to address the challenges brought about by the COVID-19 pandemic (Koaysomboon, 2020):

1. **Diversification of Services:**
    - Marriott properties had to adapt to low demand by accepting takeout and delivery orders and offering affordable long-stay packages for guests.
    - Accor provided vacant hotel rooms as makeshift offices for those seeking a quiet work environment in Bangkok, addressing the changing needs of individuals whose offices were closed.
2. **Strategic Collaboration**
    - Accor collaborated with Mövenpick BDMS Wellness Resort and Bangkok Hospital to offer a long-stay package with daily checkups, targeting those returning to Thailand from abroad for luxurious self-quarantine.
3. **Technology Integration:**
    - Anticipating increased technology adoption, both Marriott and Accor highlighted the rise in mobile check-ins, virtual room keys, and concierge apps to enhance safety and reduce physical contact. Marriott has already implemented these services in more than 3,200 hotels worldwide.
4. **Focus on Domestic and Regional Markets**
    - Accor and Marriott recognised the potential of local and regional tourism. They expected domestic travel to be the first market to rebound, focusing on attracting local markets for staycations or trips within Thailand. According to Muritala et al. (2022), although staycations and domestic tourism cannot compensate for the revenue shortfall from international tourism, this is an essential scheme to support tourism operations from bankruptcy, especially considering COVID-19 criticalities. In their study, Thailand was one of the top 20 locations for staycation searches, ranking behind Hong Kong, Singapore, and Barbados (top 3 searches).

In contrast, in September and October 2021, the UK faced a fuel crisis due to a combination of factors causing chaos at petrol pumps nationwide. Although oil companies insisted that there was enough petrol, a truck driver shortage to cover the last mile created problems. The UK was particularly affected by Brexit-related visa changes and the global COVID-19 pandemic, leading to European lorry drivers leaving the country. The pandemic also caused a backlog of new drivers awaiting tests and clearance to transport fuel. This resulted in a fuel shortage, heightened by panic buying among motorists. The UK government took resilient actions aligned with a persistence-based view of resilience to overcome the crisis. They offered short-term visas to overseas drivers, encouraged former drivers to return, and temporarily deployed military personnel to supply badly affected petrol stations. Additionally, some companies provide attractive financial packages to secure the services of drivers. These efforts aimed to alleviate the problem quickly and highlighted the importance of resilient actions in addressing disruptions within a supply chain (Davey & Macaskill, 2021; Wieland et al., 2023).

A final example for this chapter is related to transportation services. In March 2021, the Ever-Given container ship blockage in the Suez Canal caused a six-day disruption in one of the world's busiest shipping routes, impacting approximately 12% of daily global trade. Despite its brief duration, the incident led to widespread supply chain shortages, affecting industries such as automotive, medical supplies, food, homeware, and sporting goods. The response involved immediate and collaborative engineering efforts to free the blocked vessel. Tugboats and specialist boats from Europe, along with dredgers, were deployed to dislodge the ship and clear the canal. Shipping resumed on March 29, 2021, but it took until early April to clear the backlog of waiting ships. This example illustrates the vulnerability of interconnected supply chains and the need for resilient, collaborative responses to swiftly overcome disruptions and restore normal operations in the Suez Canal (BBC News, 2021; New Zealand Foreign Affairs & Trade, 2021; Wieland et al., 2023).

References

ABIT. (2020). DeMillus reconfigura fábrica para produzir máscaras e aventais para venda e doação. Retrieved from https://www.abit.org.br/noticias/demillus-reconfigura-fabrica-para-produzir-mascaras-e-aventais-para-venda-e-doacao (Last accessed: 13.03. 2024).

Acebes, F., González-Varona, J. M., & López-Paredes, A. (2024). Beyond probability-impact matrices in project risk management: A quantitative methodology for risk prioritisation. *Humanities & Social Science Communications, 11*(670), 1–13.

Airbnb. (n.d.). *Health and safety requirements for Airbnb stays*. Airbnb. Retrieved June 21, 2024, from https://www.airbnb.co.uk/help/article/2839

Akbar, B., & Aslam, H. (2023). Reinforcing resilience on the supply side: The role of supplier capabilities. *Business Process Management Journal, 29*(6), 1938–1957.

Ali, A., Mahfouz, A., & Arisha, A. (2017). Analysing supply chain resilience: Integrating the constructs in a concept mapping framework via a systematic literature review. *Supply Chain Management, 22*(1), 16–39.

Ambulkar, A., Blackhurst, J., & Grawe, S. (2015). Firm's resilience to supply chain disruptions: Scale development and empirical examination. *Journal of Operations Management, 33*(34), 111–122.

American Psychological Association (APA). (2024). Resilience. Retrieved from https://www.apa.org/topics/resilience#:~:text=Resilience%20is%20the%20process%20and,to%20external%20and%20internal%20demands (Last accessed: 13.03.2024).

Annarelli, A., Battistella, C., & Nonino, F. (2020). A framework to evaluate the effects of organizational resilience on service quality. *Sustainability, 12*(3), 958.

Azadegan, A., & Dooley, K. (2021). A typology of supply network resilience strategies: Complex collaborations in a complex world. *Journal of Supply Chain Management, 57*, 17–26.

BBC News. (2011). Foot-and-mouth outbreak of 2001. Retrieved from https://www.bbc.co.uk/news/england (Last accessed: 29.05.2024).

BBC News. (2021). Egypt's Suez Canal blocked by huge container ship. Retrieved from https://www.bbc.co.uk/news/world-middle-east-56505413 (Last accessed:13.03.2024).

Booking.com. (n.d.). *Reassuring guests with health and safety measures*. Booking.com. Retrieved June 21, 2024, from https://partner.booking.com/en-gb/solutions/advice/reassuring-guests-health-and-safety-measures

Bull, M. (2020). Holidays: New 'sanitation filter' can show how clean your hotel room is – before you book. Express – Travel News. Retrieved from https://www.express.co.uk/travel/articles/1314690/holidays-2020-travel-advice-CuddlyNest-bookings-coronavirus-pandemic-lockdown (Last accessed: 21.06. 2024).

Carvalho, H., Barroso, A. P., Machado, V. H., Azevedo, S., & Cruz-Machado, V. (2012). Supply chain redesign for resilience using simulation. *Computers & Industrial Engineering, 62*(1), 329–341.

Christopher, M., & Holweg, M. (2011). Supply Chain 2.0": Managing supply chains in the era of turbulence. *International Journal of Physical Distribution & Logistics Management, 41*(1), 63–82.

Christopher, M., & Peck, H. (2004). Building the resilient supply chain. *International Journal of Logistics Management, 15*(2), 1–14.

Costa, F. H. O., Da Silva, A. L., Pereira, C. R., Pereira, S. C. F., & Gómez Paredes, F. J. (2019). Achieving organisational resilience through inbound logistics effort. *British Food Journal, 122*(2), 432–447.

Costa, F. H. O., Moraes, C. C., Pereira, C. R., Silva, A. L., Delai, I., & Chaudhuri, A. (2022). Does resilience reduce food waste? Analysis of Brazilian supplier-retailer dyad. *Journal of Cleaner Production, 338*, 130488.

Craighead, C. W., Ketchen, D. J., Jr., & Darby, J. L. (2020). Pandemics and supply chain management research: Toward a theoretical toolbox. *Decision Sciences, 51*, 838–866.

Dabhilkar, M., Birkie, S. E., & Kaulio, M. (2016). Supply-side resilience as practice bundles: A critical incident study. *International Journal of Operations & Production Management, 36*(8), 948–970.

Darling, K. A., Kale, C., Turnage, S., Hornbuckle, B. C., Luckenbaugh, T. L., Grendahl, S., & Solanki, S. N. (2017). Nanocrystalline material with anomalous modulus of resilience and spring back effect. *Scripta Materialia, 141*, 36–40.

Davey, J., & Macaskill, A. (2021). With gas pumps still dry, Britain brings in the army. Retrieved from https://www.reuters.com/world/uk/britain-says-fuel-crisis-is-stabilising-2021-10-01/ (Last accessed: 13.03.2024).

Davis, C. (2021). Autumn 2000: When fuel shortages brought UK to virtual standstill. Retrieved from https://www.theguardian.com/business/2021/sep/23/autumn-2000-fuel-shortages-uk-standstill-price-protest-panic-buying (Last accessed: 29.05.2024).

Davis-Sramek, B., & Richey, R. G., Jr. (2021). New perspectives on supply chain resilience. *Journal of Business Logistics, 42*, 312–314.

Dwaikat, N. Y., Zighan, S., Abualqumboz, M., & Alkalha, Z. (2022). The 4Rs supply chain resilience framework: A capability perspective. *Journal of Contingencies and Crisis Management, 30*, 281–294.

Essuman, D., Ataburo, H., Boso, N., Anin, E. K., & Appiah, L. O. (2023). In search of operational resilience: How and when improvisation matters. *Journal of Business Logistics, 44*, 300–322.

Fiksel, J., Polyviou, M., Croxton, K. L., & Pettit, T. J. (2014). From risk to resilience: Learning to deal with disruption. MIT Sloan Management Review, Winter 2015. Retrieved from https://sloanreview.mit.edu/article/from-risk-to-resilience-learning-to-deal-with-disruption/ (Last accessed: 13.03.2024).

Fiksel, J. (2006). Sustainability and resilience: Toward a systems approach. *Sustainability: Science Practice and Policy, 2*(2), 14–21.

Gunderson, L. H. (2000). Ecological resilience–In theory and application. *Annual Review of Ecology and Systematics, 31*, 425–439.

Hallegatte, S. (2014). Economic Resilience: Definition and Measurement (Policy Research Working Paper No. 6852). World Bank, Washington, DC. Available at: https://documents1.worldbank.org/curated/en/350411468149663792/pdf/WPS6852.pdf. (Last accessed:13.03.2024).

Holling, C. S. (1996). *Engineering Resilience versus Ecological Resilience. In: Engineering within Ecological Constraints*. National Academies Press, Washington, DC, 224p.

Ivanov, D. (2020). Viable supply chain model: Integrating agility, resilience and sustainability perspectives—lessons from and thinking beyond the COVID-19 pandemic. *Annual Operations Research, 319*, 1411–1431.

Jackson, P. (2021). September 11 attacks: what happened on 9/11? *BBC New – US & Canada*. Available at: https://www.bbc.com/news/world-us-canada-49567955. (Last accessed:29.05.2024).

Jüttner, U., & Maklan, S. (2011). Supply chain resilience in the global financial crisis: An empirical study. *Supply Chain Management, 16*(4), 246–259.

Kamalahamadi, M., & Parast, M. M. (2016). A review of the literature on the principles of enterprise and supply chain resilience: Major findings and directions for future research. *International Journal of Production Economics, 171*, 116–133.

Karl, A. A., Micheluzzi, J., Leite, L. R., & Pereira, C. R. (2018). Supply chain resilience and key performance indicators: A systematic literature review. *Production, 28*, 1–16.

Kassem, A. M., Khoiry, M.A. and Hamzah, N. (2019). "Using probability impact matrix (PIM) in analyzing risk factors affecting the success of oil and gas construction projects in Yemen", *International Journal of Energy Sector Management*, Vol. 14 No. 3, pp. 527–546. https://doi.org/10.1108/IJESM-03-2019-0011

Kidy Calçados. (2020). Kidy Calçados se adapta na fabricação de máscaras protetivas para atender as demandas provocadas pela pandemia do Coronavírus. Available at: https://www.linkedin.com/pulse/kidy-cal%25C3%25A7ados-se-adapta-na-fabrica%25C3%25A7%25C3%25A3o-de-m%25C3%25A1scaras-para-kidy-cal%25C3%25A7ados/?trackingId=rhaVT837TFW7p0XYf4xB2Q%3D%3D. (Last accessed: 13.03.2024).

Koaysomboon, T. (2020). Accor and Marriott hotels on how to adapt to the post-pandemic tourism. Available at: https://www.timeout.com/bangkok/travel/accor-and-marriott-hotels-on-how-to-adapt-to-the-post-pandemic-tourism. (Last accessed: 13.03.2024).

Maslaric, M., Backalic, T., Nikolicic, S., & Mircetic, D. (2013). Assessing the trade-off between lean and resilience through supply chain risk management. *International Journal of Industrial Engineering and Management, 4*(4), 229–236.

Mercedes-Benz Cars & Vans Brasil. (2020). Mercedes-Benz apoia KTK e ajuda a aumentar produção para 70 respiradores mecânicos por dia. Available at: https://imprensa.mercedes-benz.com.br/releases/mercedes-benz-apoia-ktk-e-ajuda-a-aumentar-producao-para-70-respiradores-mecanicos-por-dia. (Last accessed: 13.03.2024).

Muritala, B. A., Hernández-Lara, A.-B., & Sánchez-Rebull, M.-V. (2022). COVID-19 staycations and the implications for leisure travel. *Heliyon, 8*(10), 1–12.

Nasdaq. 2020. Press Release: Arcelik continues its drive to meet mechanical ventilator demand for countries in need. Available at: https://www.nasdaq.com/press-release/arcelik-continues-its-drive-to-meet-mechanical-ventilator-demand-for-countries-in. (Last accessed: 20.06.2024).

New Zealand Foreign Affairs & Trade. (2021). The importance of the Suez Canal to Global Trade. Available at: https://www.mfat.govt.nz/en/trade/mfat-market-reports/the-importance-of-the-suez-canal-to-global-trade-18-april-2021/. (Last accessed: 13.03.2024).

Globo News. (2020). Suzano finaliza primeira etapa de desinfecção de espaços públicos: Ação visa diminuir a propagação de novo coronavírus. Diário TV, 1° Edição. Retrieved from https://g1.globo.com/sp/mogi-das-cruzes-suzano/noticia/2020/05/09/suzano-finaliza-primeira-etapa-de-desinfeccao-de-espacos-publicos.ghtml (Last accessed: 13.03.2024).

Nicácio, A., Bonfanti, C., Abreu, D. J., Queiroz, G., Boaventura, H., Milanesio, M., Rodrigues, M. J., & Mello, M. (2020). Indústria x coronavírus: como a produção brasileira se transformou para combater a pandemia. *CNI (Confederação Nacional da Indústria)*. Available at: https://noticias.portaldaindustria.com.br/especiais/especial-dia-da-industria-2020/. (Last accessed: 13.03.2024)

Novak, D. C., Wu, Z., & Dooley, K. J. (2021). Whose resilience matters? Addressing issues of scale in supply chain resilience. *Journal of Business Logistics, 42*, 323–335.

Pearson, G. (2023). Turkey and Syria earthquakes: Housing worst hit but infrastructure not immune. Infrastructure Global. Retrieved from https://infra.global/turkiye-earthquakes-housing-worst-hit-but-infrastructure-not-immune/ (Last accessed: 21.06.2024).

Pereira, C. R., Christopher, M., & Silva, A. L. (2014). Achieving supply chain resilience: The role of procurement. *Supply Chain Management: An International Journal, 19*(5/6), 626–642.

Pettit, T. J., Croxton, K. L., & Fiksel, J. (2019). The Evolution of Resilience in Supply Chain Management: A Retrospective on Ensuring Supply Chain Resilience. *Journal of Business Logistics, 40*, 56–65.

Pettit, T. J., Fiksel, J., & Croxton, K. L. (2010). Ensuring supply chain resilience: Development of a conceptual framework. *Journal of Business Logistics, 31*(1), 1–21.

Pillai, S. G., Haldorai, K., Seo, W. S., & Kim, W. G. (2021). COVID-19 and hospitality 5.0: Redefining hospitality operations. *International Journal of Hospitality Management, 94*, 102869.

Ponomarov, S. Y., & Holcomb, M. C. (2009). Understanding the concept of supply chain resilience. *International Journal of Logistics Management, 20*(1), 124–143.

Scholten, K., & Schilder, S. (2015). The role of collaboration in supply chain resilience. *Supply Chain Management: An International Journal, 20*(4), 471–484.

Sheffi, Y. (2005). *The Resilient Enterprise: Overcoming Vulnerability for Competitive Advantage*. MIT Press Books, The MIT Press, Edition 1, Volume 1, number 0262693496, December.

Sheffi, Y., & Rice, J. B., Jr. (2005). A Supply Chain View of the Resilient Enterprise. *MIT Sloan Management Review, 47*(1), 41–48.

Simchi-Levi, D., Schmidt, W., Wei, Y., Zhang, P. Y., Combs, K., Ge, Y., & Zhang, D. (2015). Identifying risks and mitigating disruptions in the automotive supply chain. *Interfaces, 45*(5), 375–390.

Simmie, J., & Martin, R. (2010). The economic resilience of regions: Towards an evolutionary approach. *Cambridge Journal of Regions, Economy and Society, 3*, 27–43.

Spiegler, V. L. M., Naim, M. M., & Wikner, J. (2012). A control engineering approach to the assessment of supply chain resilience. *International Journal of Production Research, 50*(21), 6162–6187.

THY. (2020). THY Annual Report-2020. Available at: https://investor.turkishairlines.com/documents/faaliyet-raporlari/thy_annual-report_2020.pdf (Last accessed: 22. 06. 2024).

Tukamuhabwa, B. R., Stevenson, M., Busby, J., & Zorzini, M. (2015). Supply chain resilience: Definition, review and theoretical foundations for further study. *International Journal of Production Research, 53*(18), 5592–5623.

Umar, M., & Wilson, M. M. J. (2023). Inherent and adaptive resilience of logistics operations in food supply chains. *Journal of Business Logistics, 45*, e12362.

Uno-Habitat. (2018). *Social Resilience Guide* (City Resilience Profiling Programme). Available at: https://urbanresiliencehub.org/wp-content/uploads/2018/11/Social-Resilience-Guide-SMALL-Pages.pdf. Accessed on 13 March 2024.

Urciuoli, L., Mohanty, S., Hintsa, F., & Boekesteijn, E. G. (2014). The resilience of energy supply chains: A multiple case study approach on oil and gas supply chains to Europe. *Supply Chain Management: An International Journal, 19*(1), 46–63.

Vega, D., Arvidsson, A., & Saïah, F. (2023). Resilient supply management systems in times of crisis. *International Journal of Operations & Production Management, 43*(1), 70–98.

Walker, B. (2020). Resilience: What it is and is not. *Ecology and Society, 25*(2), 11.

Wieland, A. (2020). Dancing the Supply Chain: Toward Transformative Supply Chain Management. *Journal of Supply Chain Management, 57*(1), 58–73.

Wieland, A., & Durach, C. F. (2021). Two perspectives on supply chain resilience. *Journal of Business Logistics, 42*, 315–322.

Wieland, A., Stevenson, M., Melnyk, S. A., Davoudi, S., & Schultz, L. (2023). Thinking differently about supply chain resilience: What we can learn from social-ecological systems thinking. *International Journal of Operations & Production Management, 43*(1), 1–21.

Wright, J. (2013). Taking a Broader View of. Supply Chain Management Review, March/April, 2013.

Wu, C., Cenci, J., Wang, W., & Zhang, J. (2022). Resilience city: Characterization, challenges and outlooks. *Buildings, 12*(516), 1–23.

Zsidisin, G. A., et al. (2000). Purchasing organization involvement in risk assessments, contingency plans, and risk management: an exploratory study. *Supply Chain Management, 5*(4), 187–197.

CHAPTER 5

The Role of Procurement in Achieving Service Supply Chain Resilience

Abstract In Chapter 5, we delve into the particularities of service, procurement, and resilience to understand how service supply chain resilience can be achieved through procurement actions classified into intraorganisational domains (knowledge and skills, inventory, service as solutions, and technology) and interorganisational domains (strategic sourcing, service supply chain design, transportation, and risk in service). Practical outcomes and examples from interviews conducted with professionals in service supply chain members, such as hotels, airline companies, and third-party logistics firms, are used to provide a better understanding of the domains.

Keywords Intraorganisational domains · Interorganisational domains · Service supply chain resilience

Considering the discussion on service (Chapter 2), procurement (Chapter 3), and resilience (Chapter 4) individually, let us now work on how these concepts can be combined to foster service supply chain resilience through procurement actions. In this chapter, you will learn about how procurement can promote service resilience by developing actions through intra- and interorganisation domains. To make it even

C. Pereira and Ö. Yurt, *Achieving Resilience in Service Supply Chains*, Palgrave Studies in Logistics and Supply Chain Management, https://doi.org/10.1007/978-3-031-68244-5_5

Table 5.1 General information from the interviewees

Pseudonym	Position	Service segment	Experience in service
Adam	Logistics manager	Logistics	31 years
Nigel	Hotel manager	Hotel	8 years
Tom	Data analyst for customer experience	Courier Service	7 years
Steve	Hotel director	Hotel	7 years
Tim	Logistics manager	Logistics	23 years
George	Logistics specialist	Logistics	10 years
John	Aviation operations responsible	Airline Services	11 years

more practical and easier to digest, we used interview quotes from professionals from different service segments (e.g., hotels, airlines, and logistics) to exemplify each of the key areas or activities from the domains.

Starting our reflection on Pereira et al.'s (2020) work, they noted that procurement is an essential function for supporting supply chain resilience by essentially managing and controlling ***organisational structure, risk management***, and ***knowledge acquisition and backup***. However, similar to the vast majority of the empirical research on procurement and supply chains, their study also reflects the manufacturing scope. Considering the distinctive characteristics of services, potentially different organisational structures of service companies, and their position in the supply chain, we build on it and propose adapted domains for service supply chains. Additionally, when bridging intra- and interorganisational domains, procurement must focus on crucial areas to effectively manage and coordinate the flow of services, materials, and information. In the following sections, we explore each of these critical domains and associated activities through the lens of service supply chains.

As mentioned earlier, we conducted empirical research to explore supply chain professionals' perceptions of the requirements for achieving supply chain resilience in the service sector. Table 5.1 shows the interviewees' details. For confidentiality reasons, pseudonyms are used instead of the interviewees' names.

In the following subsections, you will see relevant interview quotes that support our discussion, which were the result of open questions such as "*How can procurement managers support the creation of resilience in the service supply chain? Through what activities, roles or responsibilities?"*. The idea was to let them speak freely to share their own conclusions and insights. During the interviews, we selected key ideas and insights raised by the interviewees and questioned them further about another related topic (Salmons, 2014). We also asked a wrap-up question: *"Do you see any other potential areas in which procurement can act to develop resilience?"*.

5.1 Intraorganisational Domains

We first focus on the intraorganisational level to discuss three main domains: knowledge and skills, inventory, and service (and supplementary products) as solutions. These are areas in which procurement, as a function, should put forward actions and activities to promote service resilience.

5.1.1 Knowledge and Skills

Recognising the value of knowledge accumulated over time is critical for any organisation to improve its operations and develop proactive plans to promote readiness, competitiveness, and, consequently, growth. Creating and regularly updating databases serves as a smart tool, enabling procurement professionals to assess risks based on past experiences. Such databases should cover not only quantitative data from a series of business spreadsheets but also qualitative decisions made or staff brainstorming ideas to address or avoid different situations. This is normally the hardest piece of information that organisations do not pay attention to having records. This proactive approach not only makes it easier to address potential future issues but also instils a sense of preparedness, making the organisation more resilient and providing a solid basis for improving staff skills through training.

In line with this, Sheffi (2001, p.4) argues that *"...companies can't afford to keep redundant employees around 'just in case'; they need to ensure their knowledge is backed up"*. He categorises this backup into three areas: company processes, company knowledge, and company relationships. This view also supports the positive impact of the capacity to learn from past experiences on the management of organisational resources to persist, adapt, and transform the business.

The interviews we conducted with supply chain professionals also highlighted the importance of skills, such as communication or critical thinking, to support organisations in making the right decisions to promote resilience. In this respect, Adam (logistics manager) stated, *"People need to have some sort of skills to manage the team, to know how to deal with some sort of problems related to that area"*. This aspect has also been emphasised in the literature. Svahn and Westerlund (2009), for instance, highlight the significance of internal communication among various functions to relay information regarding product types and lead times to procurement. This ensures that the need for procurement function is well informed about the specific supplier requirements of internal customers. However, in companies with highly hierarchical organisational structures, where interdepartmental communication might be slow, the flow of information can be restricted, posing a barrier to visibility and resilience.

We can identify through the interviews how a flexible physical structure can be beneficial for improving communication. *"If I need to talk with someone from quality, I just get up from my desk, walk a few metres, and the guy from quality is sitting there. So we can go there and talk to him, and that is very, very good and helpful for aligning information" (Tim)*. Chiang et al. (2012) and Pereira et al. (2020) argue that by enhancing communication between procurement and other functions, organisations should be able to reduce costs and lead times while improving flexibility, quality, and overall competitiveness. Consequently, this facilitates organisational agility in responding to unexpected events.

The following box shows some supporting statements extracted from the interviews when practitioners were questioned about "*How can procurement managers support the creation of resilience in the service supply chain? Through what activities, roles or responsibilities?*".

> *"First of all, communication…the correct communication. And not from the top to the bottom, it's just from the side to the middle. […] Sometimes or often thinking beyond, thinking around corners and not only straight. Always have alternatives, or think about alternatives." (Adam)*

"It's a problem-solving like trying to identify what the cause is? what's causing your issue? what are the impacts? like what happens if it doesn't get fixed soon? who will be impacted? which team? what will be the business impact? And then with that you need to learn, OK, is there a business impact? Who is responsible? Who can help me? who can support? or what parts should be communicated of that because they are expecting this information or this process to?" (Tom)

"Learning from your mistakes and the ability to learn from others' mistakes. That's one skill." (Steve)

"The purchasing manager or the procurement function is also a service provider, and if they want to build resilience, the first thing they have to do is to understand this, and work very closely with the customers, the internal customers, right? Let's say it like to understand what the requirements are, what the needs are, what matters the most, what... and at the same time they are very close to the team like logistics who are going to execute this. So where you have great resilience, have very expressive results, it's usually where you have been working with group and sharing a large amount of information. But how do you do it in Purchasing where you're dealing with extremely sensitive information, like product data, sometimes data from new products that have not yet arrived on the market? You have to be careful. On the one hand, with all the data security, but on the other hand, it's a way that I think... bringing people to work with you, because you can't do everything by yourself." (Tim)

5.1.2 Inventory

Redundancy of Critical Items

Managing inventory is vital not only for manufacturing companies but also for service companies. Although the perishability characteristics of service make it impossible to stock it, service organisations need to rely on physical goods to deliver excellent service. For instance, hospitals cannot function without a reasonable stock of medicines, bed sheets, and food supplies. An inventory, or safety stock, is therefore vital to preventing a halt to operations and ensuring customer satisfaction. Christopher and Peck (2004) argue that having safety stock or a "slack" in inventory is a key way to build resilience in the supply chain. When an unexpected incident occurs, the company can easily handle it by having a small surplus of stock to maintain its resilience. This approach helps to fill gaps in material delivery, ensuring customer satisfaction through the seamless flow of not only physical products but also services and information (Akbar & Aslam, 2023).

While maintaining internal stock can be a good strategy for responding to unforeseen events, it only buys organisations extra time to find more effective solutions (Zsidisin & Wagner, 2010; Zsidisin et al., 2000). This strategy should be approached cautiously because it can increase inventory holding costs (e.g., facility expenses, invested capital, supplier management), especially for companies operating in the service sector.

Similarly to the above box, the following box provides supporting statements about the use of inventory in the service when asked the open question.

"...In 2022 we had the Commonwealth Games here in Birmingham. Around 20 - 25 different nationalities came and stayed in our hotel, so that was the fun part. But in terms of supply chain, we had obviously forecasted that there's going to be a lot more demand and you know since we had people from different countries, they had their own demands too. Somebody wanted something, somebody else wanted something else. So you know we had to keep a whole pool of inventory with us so that we could we could cater to everyone." (Nigel)

"I always try to have backups. That's all. I always try to have backups like. If this fails, I can always use the backup, but simple as that if electricity pays. So for example, if I have a backup for power supply for electricity fails, I can rely on my generator. If I always have an extra employee. So if somebody gets sick, I can use the I don't have a shortfall. I always have extra of what I need on a daily basis. Say for example linings or cleaning supplies. I always try to have extra so that if a sudden shortfall or a sudden spike in demand occurs, I don't have to have to. Deal with the. Deal with not having what I have want to have, so I plan. I learn from my mistakes. I I try to understand what occurs when it occurs, how to deal with it when it occurs so." (Steve)

"When we reopened after COVID, in terms of our in terms of our inventory we tried to stock as much as possible. We kept all our rooms clean, but you know, after that, there were a lot of challenges, especially with suppliers because they also didn't know what to expect and they also didn't know their own demand. [...] Maintaining inventory, as I said it's one of our focuses in hotels. If a customer needs something, we have to have it there." (Nigel)

Emergent Stock or Stockpiles

Unlike everyday minimal safety stock, emergent stock is reserved for extreme disruptions and their resulting needs. Companies must carefully assess whether there is a genuine need for this strategy; otherwise, maintaining it can be a costly decision. Therefore, it is important for them to focus on developing effective inventory management strategies. This is a key concern for procurement managers to enable quick responses to critical events while also allowing time for companies to find solutions. The following statement, taken from Yen et al. (2015), supports this view.

"Global vaccine stockpiles, in which vaccines are reserved for use when needed for emergencies or supply shortages, have effectively provided countries with the capacity for rapid response to emergency situations, such as outbreaks of yellow fever and meningococcal meningitis. [...] At present, four global vaccine stockpiles are maintained, mainly for emergency response situations. These include stockpiles of smallpox vaccine, meningococcal vaccine, yellow fever and oral cholera vaccines." (Yen et al., 2015, *p.1)*

Finally, the following box presents representative statements from interviewees to support the importance of emergent stock in service.

"You suddenly see a surge in occupancy. You know that they're going to come and have a few beers at your bar. So you have to stock up with your things and everything. So I would say a bit of resilience but obviously the calmness and attitude is definitely the first." (Nigel)

"I always keep one room empty. So just in case I have a very important VIP guest or someone, somebody who's I have a request from. Someone very big. Someone from the local politicians or something like that so that I can always accommodate them. So that I cannot say no to them because that's buffered. So saving something from when you need." (Steve)

5.1.3 Service (and Supplementary Products) as Solutions

By cross-functionally collaborating with other teams, procurement professionals gain early insight into new service requirements. This enables the team to work collaboratively to adapt and transform traditional services as needed.

The COVID-19 pandemic and subsequent global lockdown served as business-changing moments for countless organisations, forcing them to adapt or face extinction. Among the most common changes seen in retailers were the swift transition to online shopping and delivery services. Major retailers rapidly restructured their operations, significantly reducing delivery times from what initially took a week or more during the first wave of the pandemic. Additionally, delivery companies such as Uber Eats, Just Eat, and Deliveroo pivoted their services to meet customer needs, offering not only ready-to-eat meals but also groceries, cakes, and beverages.

In this evolving landscape, procurement plays a more reactive role once other functions have completed their tasks. This role includes identifying suppliers' capabilities (Sect. 5.2.1) or new emerging technologies that can address these requirements (Sect. 5.1.4). However, during times of upstream disruptions, this function should take on a more proactive role by monitoring unusual events, anticipating future activities, and creating new service opportunities to meet customers' needs.

The following statement is from a hotel manager who provides an interesting example of how some hotels adapt their business to continue their operations during the COVID-19 lockdown. This, therefore, came from reflection around one open question.

"Hotel shut down in January. OK, so that was the peak of COVID. The second wave was just starting at the end of the first wave. We were thinking OK, COVID is over now, we can restart the business. [...] Two months into the operations, things changed drastically. They were back-to-back lockdowns, back-to-back lockdowns. Nothing is allowed and it challenged us heavily. We did not know how to take this ahead. We had to fix the costs every month. We had salaries, we had electricity charges. We had to pay all those things, so we have to do something to cover those charges. Others will be going in the minus. So we had to look at unconventional sources, new customers, new lines. We had to approach. We had to think everything differently and then we had to go and get. We figured out a way to get the medical professionals; the only people they were allowed to be outside at that time. The nurses and the doctors. So there was a huge shortage for accommodation for those people. So we had to go and approach the government and get a contract for accommodating those people. Though he did not pay us heavily, we had enough money just to run the business so. [...] It was quite challenging and [...] I had to be more flexible." (Steve)

5.1.4 Support Technology

Technology is widely recognised as a powerful tool for sharing and disseminating information in today's world. Procurement professionals should, therefore, stay abreast of new technologies and actively seek out technological innovations to support procurement processes, which is connected to Session 5.1.1 discussion about "knowledge and skills". In this regard, George (a logistics specialist) highlights the need for "*basic computer skills*". Employing tools to facilitate communication is an effective way to enhance visibility and responsiveness during times of disruption.

In general, improving communication through technology is paramount, given its significance in identifying and responding to real-time demand. Tang (2006) recounts the case of Continental Airlines following the events of 9/11. Even before the crisis, Continental Airlines collaborated with Caleb Technologies, a technology company, to develop a decision support system aimed at swiftly reassigning crews to cover open flights and returning them to their original schedules in a cost-effective manner. This system enabled Continental Airlines to save approximately US$40 million over a five-year period from major disruptions. Numerous other examples in the literature highlight the effectiveness of various methods or tools, such as simulations (Azevedo et al., 2013; Carvalho et al., 2012; Christopher & Holweg, 2011), big data analytics (Althabatah et al., 2023), artificial intelligence and the Internet of Things (Althabatah et al., 2023; Bienhaus & Haddud, 2018; Hendriksen, 2023), barcodes and RFID (Tang, 2006), blockchain and omnichannel (Min et al., 2019) or shipment visibility systems (Sheffi & Rice, 2005). The use of these tools enables faster rerouting and resolution of transportation and supply delivery issues.

Furthermore, gym classes were brought into people's homes mainly after COVID-19 through various apps. For instance, Orange Theory, Planet Fitness, and 24-Hour Fitness began streaming exercise classes online and sharing homework plans. Even the fitness clothing brand Under Armour initiated a "30-day Healthy at Home challenge" to encourage people to stay active (Morgan, 2020).

In the service sector, depending on the type of service and the size of the organisation, technologies may differ considerably. The interviewees reported different supporting technologies for airlines and logistics, mostly focused on tracking (visibility) and communication. Although technology can threaten human labour (as in Nigel's perception below), it is important to highlight that not all businesses use highly complex technologies. For instance, hotel managers have noted the use of AI-related technology to support demand forecasting. However, daily business tasks are mainly based on Excel spreadsheets.

> *"Obviously we know we're now with AI and, you know, machine learning and all these, all these things coming in. If there is a central procurement system that procures everything that procures linen, that procures food and all the things. Tomorrow we might not need any managers. We might need, you know, just people, sort of fulfilling and serving." (Nigel)*

"For supply chain management, if you can know with high level of quality and accuracy when your cargo is it a truck vessel train is going to arrive and if that is real time based... [...] marine traffic apps normally provide support" (George)

5.2 Interorganisational Domains

Following the discussion on intraorganisational domains, we now focus on the interorganisational level to discuss four remaining domains: strategic sourcing, service supply chain design, transportation modes, and risks in service. As previously highlighted, procurement should act and engage in activities to promote service resilience in these areas.

5.2.1 Strategic Sourcing

There has been extensive discussion regarding the optimal number of suppliers that companies should maintain relationships with, weighing the advantages and disadvantages of each approach. It is evident, however, that relying solely on one supplier can pose a risk to companies and their downstream partners, leaving them without a short-term alternative in the event of an unforeseen incident. Nevertheless, this strategy has also proven beneficial in reducing costs and improving quality (Christopher & Peck, 2004). Frederico (2021) emphasises the importance of having a dependable supplier over having multiple suppliers that lack quality and reliability in sharing information and experiences.

Hence, having multiple sources of suppliers is viewed as a favourable option. It can lower costs, mitigate failures, and offer sourcing flexibility, which is an essential factor in resilience (Pereira et al., 2020). The downside of this strategy is that maintaining multiple suppliers may increase supply risks, such as quality issues or delivery reliability, particularly for critical components. Additionally, managing multiple suppliers may incur higher costs. Thus, determining the appropriate number of suppliers is a key aspect of supplier management and, consequently, resilience development.

The following representative interviews' quotes are interesting for identifying the ideal number of suppliers for service companies to address different kinds of unexpected situations and improve operational performance.

"...Managers create resilience in the service sector by having multiple suppliers for each and every [product or service]. Demand that they have not sticking to, or not relying upon one single supplier. Say, for example, I have a requirement to buy linings like pillow covers, bedspreads, and blankets. I have to change them every year, though I try to stay with one particular supplier. I always have a backup. I always get quotations from different other suppliers. So just in case if this guy is not able to supply it on time to me, I can go to them. So, the ability to think. For the unthinkable, that is one thing." (Steve)

"...One of our main food supplier... they decided to help us during the busy time. Usually, we have only one delivery or two maximum 2 deliveries if we need in a week. ...they were also pretty resilient in delivering 3 times." (Nigel)

"I try to get the best solutions to get the correct supplier or the correct logistics service provider to fulfil." (Adam)

Procurement functions may aim to reduce their supply bases to be more efficient in selecting and managing supplier relationships, in addition to being able to improve relationships by working closely with suppliers. This, therefore, will depend on how strategic the items are. In this case, as discussed in Chapter 3 (Sect. 3.1.3—supply management), the Kraljic matrix is usually a common tool for organisations to classify, prioritise, and develop contingency plans. Key criteria are normally analysed by procurement professionals to identify the right resource and, consequently, select appropriate suppliers, such as supplier locations, processes, practices and culture, common platforms for products, capacity constraints, financial stability, and effectiveness of the supplier's management team.

The type of relationship between a buyer and supplier can also be analysed using the Kraljic matrix (Kraljic, 1983). For example, when a single supplier possesses the skills and capacity to provide a specific and strategic item (posing a high risk to the organisation), a close relationship is recommended. Conversely, when there are multiple suppliers for noncritical items (posing low risk to the organisation), a less intimate relationship is suitable for spreading risks and reducing costs. Nevertheless, regardless of the circumstances, fostering a good relationship between buyers and suppliers always encourages collaboration, alignment, and visibility.

Finally, developing their suppliers' capabilities to make their company more responsive during disruptions becomes a potential aim for procurement managers. When a company supports its suppliers in improving their processes, they become better aligned and more adaptable to changes. This not only enhances information sharing and integration but also increases flexibility. Working closely with suppliers in these ways helps companies better meet specific customer quality requirements. Therefore, supplier development has been shown to positively impact supplier performance and, consequently, resilience in the chain. This is potentially a more critical tool in service settings because both service buyers and service providers cocreate service production.

However, when there is no supplier available in the market to cover the company's needs, procurement should create incentives for those interested and hence take advantage and develop additional suppliers for its own business. In this context, COVID-19, again, brings good examples and lessons learned, as governments from different countries have proposed a wide range of incentives to pharmaceutical companies to develop the most expected and desired vaccine in recent years. Another recent example is the UK government incentives after BREXIT to resolve issues related to skills and job shortages; for instance, HGV drivers are still working during the COVID-19 pandemic (UK Government, n.d.).

5.2.2 *Service Supply Chain Design*

Supply chain design is one of the activities in which procurement managers should pay attention to building resilience. Christopher et al. (2011) suggest that companies, in general, are knowledgeable when the matter is downstream of the supply chain; however, this is not so true regarding the upstream side. Therefore, they claim that companies embedded in a global context should redesign their supply chains to avoid current risks in the organisational environment. Although this was highlighted a few years ago, the strong focus on the customer side (which is the main player in supply chains) tends to reduce the attention organisations give to facts at the very upstream of the chain.

Although the design of the supply chain can be the result of companies' choices regarding strategic sourcing, there are also cases in which redesign is required to mitigate risk and create a more resilient supply chain, especially in service settings. In such cases, companies are likely to compromise the goal of keeping costs low. However, it is inevitable for managers to face trade-offs in decision-making, where optimising one aspect often requires compromising another to achieve a balanced and efficient overall system. In any case, contingency plans related to supplier locations can always be an interesting strategy to be flexible and adaptable in times of crisis.

Once again, the box below holds key statements from interviewees related to how important it is to know the location partners, as well as your own location, compared to key places to support your operations.

"We know we obviously have worked out a plan that we need to order more or we need to keep X amount of stock. In terms of food, we often run out of food, but you know, fortunately, there is our Plan B, which is just to go to the nearest supermarket and get what we need." (Nigel)

"In terms of hotel rooms, you know, we've often heard that the hotel is, you know, 90% occupied, 95% occupied. But there are times our hotel has been 110% occupied as well...because on X [a third party is mentioned here] website you can book 7 rooms at once. So, what has happened is that we have been overbooked sometimes, so there was such a lot of demand we couldn't guess how much demand there is, and somebody has just booked 7 rooms on X. Due to a glitch on the system it says you can book up to 7 rooms. So that's what exactly happened. So that is another sort of inventory management that we do. So if that happens, obviously we don't panic, we go to the nearest hotel, and we ask them. First of all we ask the hotel next door do you have any rooms? They obviously quote a ridiculous amount to us and say that, oh, yeah, of course we have rooms, but we will go double sometimes. We said OK, you know we have to do that." (Nigel)

5.2.3 Transportation Modes

Depending on the organisation's structure, procurement can play a pivotal role in determining the modes of transportation (e.g., road, rail, air, sea, or multimodal) to carry and deliver raw materials and/or any other types of resources. Identifying the appropriate one is a priority for ensuring efficient and cost-effective supply chain operations. While logistics primarily handles any matter related to transportation, it is usually procurement that strategically determines how these essential components will be sourced and delivered to the company, ultimately impacting the overall operational effectiveness, profitability, and supply chain resilience accordingly.

To achieve a smooth flow of service processes along the supply chain or to be capable of dealing with unpredictable events, having more than one mode of transportation is crucial to achieving resilience. In this sense, procurement managers (from any service business) will need to have in mind or identify available options to succeed in situations such as transporting medical supplies or people to hospitals after the earthquake in Turkey and Syria, or Amazon fleet having to deal with the UK fuel shortage, or the example reported by the interviewed logistics manager (in the box below).

"We had disruptions in harbours, for example. Strikes in Santos at some point and then our vessels got stuck there and then we could not move that because that was the first destination and then was Santos, Argentina and then back to Itapoa. So, our whole lead time will be highly affected because of that strike incentives. So once the strike was released, instead of doing the normal route back to Argentina and then back to Itapoa, we had to unload our containers in Santos and then change the transportation mode from sea to road and then we drove all the containers by truck to Itapoa so we could at least still customs cleared. Santa Catarina territory and then use our tax benefits and then move from top up to our site." (Tim)

5.2.4 *Risks in Service*

The relationship between risk management and resilience has been mentioned in several parts of this pivot, and it is a well-discussed link in the literature in which risk management is one of the elements of building resilience. Here, we focus on the close relationship between the concepts of supply chain risk management and procurement actions. Identifying the sources of supply chain risk is an important issue that procurement should be aware of to enhance supply chain resilience (Pereira et al., 2020). Although the risks from suppliers must be observed before any selection, procurement should also be concerned about internal, external, and environmental risks, which have been rising in today's business, as observed in Chapter 2.

As suggested by Christopher et al. (2011), before developing strategies for managing risk, the first step for procurement managers is to understand the root causes and types of global sourcing risks. This is even highlighted by Colicchia et al., (2010, p. 692), who state that "*a better understanding of the risk sources for specific supply chain settings can enable the design of a more resilient supply chain*", which is another domain addressed in this subsection. Therefore, by identifying the sources of risk and their effects on business, procurement, in addition to other functions, should become a more prepared function for managing those risks and hence addressing and overcoming any critical situations.

In regard to service supply chains, risk management strategies for services must be determined by prioritising unique factors, such as allowing downstream members (e.g., retailers, restaurants or hotels) to coordinate the chain (Demirkan & Cheng, 2008), giving increased importance to customers and clarifying their demands in terms of value requirements (Arlbjørn et al., 2011) and considering proactive approaches to risk identification, analysis, and control (Vilko & Ritala, 2014). The following interview quotes report on these key points of attention and reflection on the likely risk, impact, and mitigation actions.

Finally, the box below illustrates two supporting statements from interviewees related to risk management in service.

"....In the aviation, we have bronze, silver and gold commands, which, whenever there's a minor event, then the bronze command would be triggered, and then you get operator. You get like duty managers from different departments that sit in a room and discuss how to manage the challenge. And then, if it's a particularly big challenge, they then go to Silver Command, where I get the next level up of managers who discuss what's the best course of action. And then for really serious events, they have gold command which is where the heads of all the different departments get together in one specific room, the CEO's there and together they all like form a plan of action. So I say that's a form of resilience and risk management as well." (John)

"It was more related to cyber security. There was some like big scandal like big leaks... we had to act fast. ... Who are the suppliers? Do we need to contact the suppliers to see if they already fixed that or? Are they still vulnerable? So there was a very big disruption, and we were able to manage well by like quickly reacting and getting the data that we need. We had that ready so we could find who to reach, who are the software that we like, what the software we use, who are the providers, who are the right contact from that like companies and then could quickly release some communications, collect some information and assess everything." (Tom)

References

Akbar, B., & Aslam, H. (2023). Reinforcing resilience on the supply side: The role of supplier capabilities. *Business Process Management Journal, 29*(6), 1938–1957.

Althabatah, A., Yaqot, M., Menezes, B., & Kerbache, L. (2023). Transformative procurement trends: Integrating Industry 4.0 technologies for enhanced procurement processes. *Logistics, 7*(3), 63.

Arlbjørn, J. S., Freytag, P. V., & Haas, H. D. (2011). Service supply chain management: A survey of lean application in the municipal sector. *International Journal of Physical Distribution & Logistics Management, 41*(3), 277–295.

Azevedo, S., Govindan, K., Carvalho, H., & Cruz-Machado, V. (2013). Ecosilient Index to assess the greenness and resilience of the upstream automotive supply chain. *Journal of Cleaner Production, 56*, 131–146.

Bienhaus, F., & Haddud, A. (2018). Procurement 4.0: factors influencing the digitisation of procurement and supply chains. *Business Process Management Journal, 24*(4), 965–984.

Carvalho, H., Azevedo, S. G., & Cruz-Machado, V. (2012). Agile and resilient approaches to supply chain management: Influence on performance and competitiveness. *Logistics Research, 4*(1–2), 49–62.

Chiang, C., Kocabasoglu-Hillmer, C., & Suresh, N. (2012). An empirical investigation of the impact of strategic sourcing and flexibility on firm's supply chain agility. *International Journal of Operations & Production Management, 32*(1), 49–78.

Christopher, M., & Holweg, M. (2011). Supply Chain 2.0: managing supply chains in the era of turbulence. *International Journal of Physical Distribution & Logistics Management, 41*(1), 63–82.

Christopher, M., Mena, C., Khan, O., & Yurt, O. (2011). Approaches to managing global sourcing risk. *Supply Chain Management: An International Journal, 16*(2), 67–81.

Christopher, M., & Peck, H. (2004). Building the Resilient Supply Chain. *International Journal of Logistics Management, 15*(2), 1–14.

Colicchia, C., Dallari, F., & Melacini, M. (2010). Increasing supply chain resilience in a global sourcing context. *Production Planning & Control, 21*(7), 680–694.

Demirkan, H., & Cheng, H. K. (2008). The risk and information sharing of application services supply chain. *European Journal of Operational Research, 187*(3), 765–784.

Frederico, G. F. (2021). Rethinking strategic sourcing during disruptions: A resilience-driven process contribution to knowledge on supply chains. *Knowledge and Process Management: THe Journal of Corporate Transformation, 30*, 83–86.

Hendriksen, C. (2023). Artificial intelligence for supply chain management: Disruptive innovation or innovative disruption? *Journal of Supply Chain Management, 59*(3), 65–76.

Kraljic, P. (1983). Purchasing must become supply management. *Harvard Business Review*, (September–October, 1983), pp. 110–117.

Min, S., Zacharia, Z. G., & Smith, C. D. (2019). Defining Supply Chain Management: In the Past, Present, and Future. *Journal of Business Logistics, 40*, 44–55.

Morgan, B. (2020). 10 examples of how COVID-19 forced business transformation. Forbes. Retrieved from https://www.forbes.com/sites/blakemorgan/2020/05/01/10-examples-of-how-covid-19-forced-business-transformation/ (Last accessed: 21.06.2024).

Pereira, C. R., da Silva, A. L., Tate, W. L., & Christopher, M. (2020). Purchasing and supply management (PSM) contribution to supply-side resilience. *International Journal of Production Economics, 228*, 107740.

Salmons, J. (2014). *Qualitative online interviews: Strategies, design, and skills* (2nd ed.). SAGE Publications Ltd.

Sheffi, Y. (2001). Supply Chain Management under the Threat of International Terrorism. *International Journal of Logistics Management, 12*(2), 1–11.

Sheffi, Y., & Rice, J. B., Jr. (2005). A Supply Chain View of the Resilient Enterprise. *MIT Sloan Management Review, 47*(1), 41–48.

Svahn, S., & Westerlund, M. (2009). Purchasing strategies in supply relationships. *Journal of Business & Industrial Marketing, 24*(3), 173–181.

Tang, C. S. (2006). Robust strategies for mitigating supply chain disruptions. *International Journal of Logistics Research and Applications: A Leading Journal of Supply Chain Management, 9*(1), 33–45.

UK Government. (n.d.). HGV driver shortage: UK government response. Retrieved from https://www.gov.uk/government/topical-events/hgv-driver-shortage-uk-government-response/about#:~:text=Providing%20support%20and%20training%20for%20new%20HGV%20drivers,-We%20invested%20%C2%A3&text=We%20gave%20an%20incentive%20payment,5%2C000%20of%20funding%20for%20training (Last accessed: 21.06.2024).

Vilko, J., & Ritala, P. (2014). Service supply chain risk management. *Operations and Supply Chain Management: An International Journal, 7*(3), 114–120.

Yen, C., Hyde, T. B., Costa, A. J., Fernandez, K., Tam, J. S., Hugonnet, S., & Burkholder, B. T. (2015). The development of global vaccine stockpiles. *The Lancet Infectious Diseases, 15*(3), 340–347.

Zsidisin, G. A., et al. (2000). Purchasing organization involvement in risk assessments, contingency plans, and risk management: An exploratory study. *Supply Chain Management, 5*(4), 187–197.

Zsidisin, G. A., & Wagner, S. M. (2010). Do perceptions become reality? The moderating role of supply chain resiliency on disruption occurrence. *Journal of Business Logistics, 31*(2), 1–20.

CHAPTER 6

Practical Insights and Guidelines

Abstract Chapter 6 revisits the key domains discussed in Chapter 5, together with key insights from the other chapters, to offer practical highlights and guidelines on how procurement management can support service professionals in better managing their supply chain processes and making their systems more resilient. These domains are the basis for procurement to efficiently oversee and synchronise the flow of services, materials, information, and related activities.

Keywords Intraorganisational domains · Interorganisational domains · Service supply chain resilience · Skills and competencies · Practical insights and guidance

In this final chapter, we revisit the key domains discussed in Chapter 5, along with takeaways from other chapters, to offer practical insights into building resilience in service supply chains through the procurement function. These domains are the basis for procurement to efficiently oversee and synchronise the flow of services, materials, information, and related activities.

C. Pereira and Ö. Yurt, *Achieving Resilience in Service Supply Chains*, Palgrave Studies in Logistics and Supply Chain Management,
https://doi.org/10.1007/978-3-031-68244-5_6

According to the key findings of Pereira et al. (2020), procurement is seen as the key function for effectively managing and controlling the discussed domains in three areas: *organisational structure, risk management*, and *knowledge acquisition and backup*. These findings are important elements to consider. However, service businesses require a distinct focus and configuration due to their intangible characteristics. For instance, as one of our interviewees' comments, the organisational structure for service businesses tends to be highly flexible and customer-driven. "*If I need to talk with someone from the Quality department, I just get up from my desk, walk a few metres, and the guy from Quality is sitting there. So we can go there and talk to him, and that is very, very good and helpful for aligning information*" (George, logistics specialist). While service procurement should involve direct contact with suppliers, we observed through practitioners' interviews that they are also close to customers, as they need to understand their preferences and expectations.

For example, the interviewed hotel manager and director stated that they have a comprehensive understanding of their business (spanning from end to end), which helps them make procurement decisions based on the knowledge they have been acquiring over the years about customers and the hospitality market. In this sense, we understand that the main resource for achieving service supply chain resilience is human factors or professionals within service businesses. The relevant *knowledge* and the learning opportunities they have is key to nourish the organisation's expertise in persisting, adapting, and transforming their operations when dealing with different sources of disruptions. John mentioned the following:

> *"I say the second one is knowledge of the system itself. Because you can change the plans without the knowledge. But I think a more effective decision would be made if you had overall knowledge of how the wider system works rather than just your tiny little part of it."*

Additionally, their openness to learn with customers and make their service "as a product", as well as the efficient communication flow they must sustain in the organisation (through training sessions, for instance), influence the development and enrichment of the organisational knowledge package among professionals. This reveals another critical aspect—the *distinctive skills* that are required for supply chain professionals in the service sector. At this point, we should highlight that there still exists a critical challenge for supply chain managers, as pointed out by Christopher (2023) as the "T-shaped skills profile". This notion mainly addresses the hybrid nature of skills that supply chain professionals have. For instance, a service supply chain professional may be well trained and equipped with service processes and management (in which they have *in-depth expertise*), but they should also have a significant *(breadth of)* understanding of supply chain processes. Therefore, future procurement professionals in service sectors should be equipped with both skills to be capable of managing disruptions in dynamic markets and global sourcing risks and, at the same time, enhancing future supply chain resilience. Tom makes a relevant point here:

> *"I remember a project when I was working for procurement, and what we were doing was like mapping all these skills required for each individual, like on different levels of the career but also on different teams. And then we are ranking this like so, for example, each role on different levels, they need to have some set of skills and then some skills you don't need to learn how to apply like you, it's enough if you'll learn how it works. You don't need to apply, but you need to understand the concepts. […] So for data and reporting and this kind of things, I need to know much more than a person that's only like getting the results of that or not using it on their daily basis. And then the last level you need to know."*

Bringing back the skills and competencies highlighted in Chapter 3, Table 6.1 provides some insights into how those skills and competencies could be applied to different segments of the service sector. These insights are based on a combination of theoretical findings and feedback from interviewees.

Although more research is needed in this area to explore the key distinctive skills and competencies for procurement managers in service supply chains, our primary findings show that particular attention must be given to how different skills should be developed in service supply chain professionals to consider all the domains discussed in this study and strategically combine and manage them. We propose Fig. 6.1 as a guide to show the relationships between the different proposed domains.

Efforts and investments should start with developing and sustaining *"knowledge and skills"* among procurement professionals. In promoting this, informed internal actions will be taken on "*inventory management*", "*support technology*", and *"service (and supplementary products) as solutions"*. Having this foundation, procurement professionals will then delve

Table 6.1 Insights into skills and competencies for procurement professionals in service

Skills and competencies	*How could this be applied?*	*How could this support the development of resilience?*
Communication Skills	- Organise regular meetings with staff to clarify changes and new procedures - Encourage free communication by allowing staff to share their insights and concerns without fearing to be judged - Implement feedback mechanisms (e.g., suggestion boxes and surveys)	Promoting transparent and effective communication between and among stakeholders to support updated or real-time information sharing and alignment of resources, order, goals, and expectations
Problem-solving	- Identify potential risks and mitigation actions (e.g., through brainstorming sessions or kaizen cycles) through regular risk assessment analysis and scenario planning - Actively seek customers' feedback on their preferences, expectations, and satisfaction to improve operations. Additionally, ask for their suggestions on solutions and improvements	Understanding business risks and opportunities to increase customer satisfaction and loyalty promotes business alignment, increases the company's knowledge, and strategically designs a flexible and resilient supply chain

Skills and competencies	*How could this be applied?*	*How could this support the development of resilience?*
Strategic Thinking	- Continuously monitor market trends to adapt operations and align them with organisational goals - Develop new business streams (e.g., renting main rooms for conferences or celebration events, opening up spas and gyms, or identifying the town's events and needs for support) - Create packages and partnerships with local businesses to attract customers, creating a win–win strategy	Monitoring trends and opportunities in order to develop new strategies. This helps improve collaboration between partners and consequently promotes supply chain integration. As a result, this tends to increase agility and business process adaptation during disruptions
Risk Management and Awareness	- Regularly monitor risks, market trends, and global events to evaluate business scenarios and potentially identify or develop new mitigation actions - Regularly update the risk assessment analysis and contingency plans - Develop new contingency plans by addressing business vulnerabilities and potential opportunities to increase service scope and market share - Debrief and train staff on emergency response protocols	This is essentially one of the domains to promote resilience, as discussed in Chapter 5

(continued)

Table 6.1 (continued)

Skills and competencies	*How could this be applied?*	*How could this support the development of resilience?*
Negotiation Skills	- Train staff in negotiating cost savings, mutual benefits, shared risk and resources, flexible policies, insurance claims, government assistance, and any other topic that may be important for the business	Strong negotiation skills are essential for securing collaboration with suppliers, process coordination and control, and dealing with complex arrangements, ultimately promoting smooth operations and resilience
Supplier Relationship Management	- Intensively evaluate suppliers' capabilities and operations through key performance measurement analysis - Monitor potential risk of suppliers' bankruptcy or any other critical supply risk to be acted on in advance so as to mitigate - Work closely with suppliers to build and maintain solid relationships, promoting trust, coordination, operations alignment, and consequent agility in response	This is embedded in strategic sourcing, which is one of the domains that promotes resilience, as discussed in Chapter 5

Skills and competencies	*How could this be applied?*	*How could this support the development of resilience?*
Technology Proficiency and Data Analytics	- Make use of data analytics to monitor key performance indicators (KPIs) and identify new trends - Use data insights to make informed decisions and anticipate potential problems - Develop training sessions about procurement technologies, such as e-procurement systems and supply chain management software, to enhance efficiency and visibility - Identify new support technologies for forecasting, booking, or any other key business operations to optimise time and cost - Identify and implement automation tools to handle routine tasks, allowing staff to focus on more complex problem-solving activities - Explore new customer relationship management systems to understand and serve them better, fostering loyalty - Adopt integrated and user-friendly technologies to reduce the amount of time invested in staff training for new technologies. Fewer and more integrated technologies tend to be better than using many separate systems - Consider technologies and implications (e.g. facilitate remote work and virtual collaboration) to adapt to new ways of working and keep operations running during disruptions (e.g. COVID-19)	This is also embedded in strategic sourcing, which is one of the domains that promotes resilience, as discussed in Chapter 5

(continued)

Table 6.1 (continued)

Skills and competencies	*How could this be applied?*	*How could this support the development of resilience?*
Ethical and Sustainable Procurement	- Search for and implement sustainable practices (e.g., waste reduction and energy efficiency) to reduce operational costs and support ecosystem preservation and new policy regulations - Adherence to ethical standards and the ability to ensure that procurement practices align with corporate social responsibility and sustainability goals	Actions towards ethical and sustainable procurement help build trust through long-term contracts, promote supplier diversity, which secures supply, and contribute to society's cultural change, in which resilience is one of the key aspired aspects
Regulatory Compliance	- Maintain emergency funds or insurance to effectively respond and mitigate negative impacts during disruptions by enduring compliance with relevant laws, regulations, and industry standards	This supports the financial aspects of resilience, which is fundamental for business survival although not an inexpensive strategy

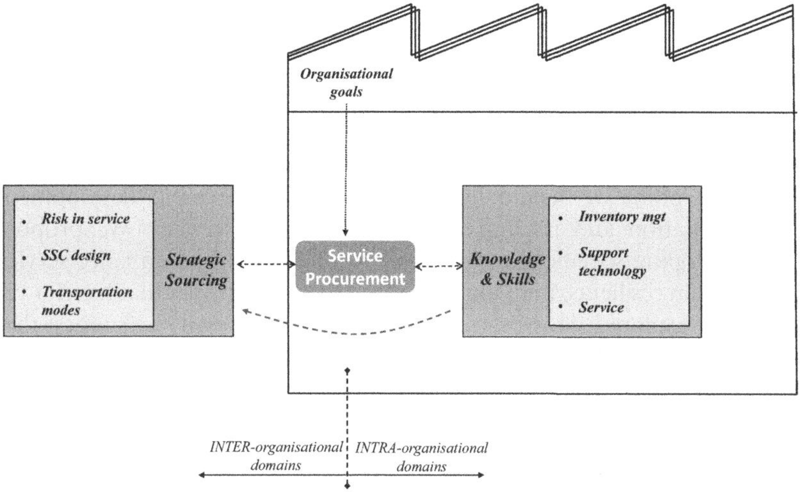

Fig. 6.1 Key areas of procurement that support the creation of SSC

into analysis around *"strategic sourcing"*, which generally covers *"risks in service"*, *"service supply chain design", and "transportation modes"*. This framework focuses on the procurement function and provides a viewpoint to supply chain professionals on how to manage service processes, both inside their organisations and within and between their supply chain partners. Supply chain professionals can use this framework as a guideline to identify the main checkpoints for designing and managing a resilient sourcing system in service settings by asking themselves how they can achieve supply chain resilience by examining each of these domains.

Another practical insight for procurement managers is about understanding the requirements for customer satisfaction in service settings as well as the challenges they face. Sampson (2000, p.348) provides a basis for this view by highlighting that *"…with service organisations, one of the primary suppliers of process inputs is customers themselves, who provide their bodies, minds, belongings, or information as inputs to the service processes"*. They call this *"customer-supplier duality"*. The following quote stressed by one of the interviewees highlights the criticality of this for a supply chain professional.

"In the service industry, the customer is the king. Accept it! The faster you accept, the better it gets, though. You might be the owner, or you might be the landlord. You might be whatever it is. It is your establishment. The faster you recognise, the faster you accept that the customer is the king. [...] Service is all about customers." (Steve)

A final point we would like to highlight is the rapid development of digitalisation and its impact on procurement services. We propose that developing specific strategies for *Procurement 4.0* to enhance service supply chain resilience is an important future research area that has not yet been fully explored. However, from a practical viewpoint, we suggest that supply chain managers keep these two aspects in mind and assess them within the T-shaped skills profile of service supply chain professionals.

References

Christopher, M. (2023). *Logistics and supply chain management*. Pearson UK.

Pereira, C. R., da Silva, A. L., Tate, W. L., & Christopher, M. (2020). Purchasing and supply management (PSM) contribution to supply-side resilience. *International Journal of Production Economics, 228*, 107740.

Sampson, S. E. (2000). Customer-supplier duality and bidirectional supply chains in service organizations. *International Journal of Service Industry Management, 11*(4), 348–364.

Index

C. Pereira and Ö. Yurt, *Achieving Resilience in Service Supply Chains*, Palgrave Studies in Logistics and Supply Chain Management,
https://doi.org/10.1007/978-3-031-68244-5

The manufacturer's authorised representative in the EU is Springer
Nature Customer Service Centre GmbH, Europaplatz 3, 69115 Heidelberg,
Germany. If you have any concerns regarding our products, please
contact ProductSafety@springernature.com

Printed and bound by CPI Group (UK) Ltd, Croydon, CR0 4YY
01/10/2026
02225879-0004